MY FAMILY TREE

An Odyssey from Virginia to Britain

Grace McLean Moses
(1908-1996), a Virginia Descendent of

John Lewis, Welsh Emigrant
from Monmouthshire to Gloucester
(1592-1657)

with Roots in Wales, England, Scotland,
Ireland and France

Edward Merillat Moses
Compiler, Author, and Researcher

Grace McLean Moses (1908–1996)
Genealogist and Researcher

HERITAGE BOOKS
2019

HERITAGE BOOKS
AN IMPRINT OF HERITAGE BOOKS, INC.

Books, CDs, and more—Worldwide

For our listing of thousands of titles see our website
at
www.HeritageBooks.com

Published 2019 by
HERITAGE BOOKS, INC.
Publishing Division
5810 Ruatan Street
Berwyn Heights, Md. 20740

Copyright © 2003 by Edward Merillat Moses Trust
Edward M. Moses, Trustee

— Publisher's Notice —
If you purchased this as a new book and the CD-Rom is missing, please contact Heritage Books
email: Orders@HeritageBooks.com
phone: 1-800-876-6103 - Customer Service Ext 1

All rights reserved. No part of this book may be reproduced or transmitted in any form or by any means, electronic or mechanical, including photocopying, recording or by any information storage and retrieval system without written permission from the author, except for the inclusion of brief quotations in a review.

International Standard Book Numbers
Paperbound: 978-1-58549-928-1
Clothbound: 978-0-7884-9406-2

DEDICATION

This book and its CD, *My Family Tree*, with our family's genealogical data are dedicated to my mother, Grace McLean Moses, who spent over forty years of her life searching for the truth of her family's origins. She started with little information, but doggedly pursued her objective. In the course of her work, she wrote a book, with a supplement, that disproved the published conclusions of a widely accepted genealogical study of the Lewis family in Gloucester, Virginia. She established with a rigor that defied dispute that the Warner Hall Lewis family's true emigrant ancestor was not one Robert Lewis, but rather was John Lewis (1592-1657), an emigrant to Gloucester County from Monmouthshire, Wales. She connected her Tidewater Virginia family to this emigrant John Lewis, and firmly established her family's ancestral lines back to ancient Wales, Ireland, and England. She also established several other historically important family connections, including a Washington family line, and traced these lines back to the early English and Scottish kings, William the Conqueror, Emperor Charlemagne, and the Roman Empire.

Grace McLean Moses invested a large part of her life and energies on behalf of our family, so that we would know from whence we came. Now we have only to reach out, read, and be proud. My mother was a most remarkable woman. Her many valuable contributions to our family, not only in the understanding of our roots, but also in many other important areas, remain indelibly locked in my memory. Too few of us leave behind in this world something of lasting value. Grace McLean Moses has certainly done that. All of my efforts on this book and its accompanying CD are dedicated to her with my heartfelt thanks for having given me this wonderful opportunity.

INTRODUCTION

This book and its accompanying CD data would not have been possible were it not for the diligent and dedicated labors of Grace McLean Moses over a forty year period between 1950 and 1990. During that time, she acquired an extensive personal genealogical library while pursuing her family's roots. She also became a very accomplished professional genealogist, and at different times she employed several other genealogists located in this country, Britain, and Wales. Two were used extensively in Wales. In the early 1980's she journeyed to Wales with her son Edward, where she acquired a sole copy of the *"Parish Register"* of St. Teilo's church, located in the county of Monmouthshire. Entries in the *"Parish Register"* began in the year 1591/92 (Old Style), and on the first page of this register is entered the baptism of **"John, son of Lewis Rycketts, February 10th, 1591/92"**. This John is our family's emigrant ancestor John Lewis, whose tombstone with the engraved **Rhys Goch, Lord of Ystrad**, coat-of-arms was discovered in Gloucester County, Virginia. In 1984, Grace Moses authored a book entitled *"The Welsh Lineage of John Lewis (1592-1657), Emigrant to Gloucester, Virginia"*, with a subsequent *"Supplement"* printed in 1988 containing corrections and addenda. This book with supplement is still in print and is published by the Clearwater Company in Baltimore, MD. Until this book was published, the emigrant ancestor of the Lewis family of Virginia, whose descendent was *"Councilor"* John Lewis III of Warner Hall, was generally believed to be one Robert Lewis. However, her research and book established beyond any doubt that the real Lewis family emigrant ancestor was in fact John Lewis of Gloucester, Virginia. Since 1984 this John Lewis has been widely accepted by other genealogists as the true Lewis family emigrant. It was in the family cemetery of the Emigrant John Lewis of Gloucester that his tombstone, engraved with a coat-of-arms, was tardily discovered. This important discovery led Grace Moses back into Wales from Virginia. From Monmouthshire in Wales, John Lewis had been exiled to Barbados by Oliver Cromwell following the great Civil War. Two years later, he immigrated to Gloucester County, Virginia, after receiving *"head rights"* of 250 acres for five persons, himself and other persons who accompanied him.

During the 1960's and for the next thirty years, Grace Moses was a frequent visitor to the Library of Congress, the National Archives, and the library of the Daughters of the American Revolution. Her personal library, which she gradually purchased in the pursuit of her family's genealogy, is probably matched by few in this country. This library is now in the possession of her son, Edward M. Moses. Grace Moses was a member of many historical and genealogical organizations. At one time she was the genealogist for the Society of the Lees. She was a member of the Jamestown Society; Regent of the Freedom Hill Chapter of the DAR; Division Historian of the United Daughters of the Confederacy; and a member of the Virginia Historical Society. She was also a member of the Daughters of Colonial Wars; the National Society of Colonial Dames XVII Century; the Barons of Runnemeade; the Magna Charta Society; Dames of the Court of Honor; and the Colonial Order of the Crown, descendent of Charlemagne. Her credentials have been examined by many organizations and they are well established.

The work documented herein is a compilation of the research by Grace Moses and an expansion of that research by her son, Edward M. Moses. He has utilized her extensive personal library; her copious notes; what is perhaps the most powerful current computer program available- *The Master Genealogist (version four and version five);* and sixty-five years of his own personal memory of her life and work. This book records the results of the forty years of research by includes 5,339 people; 15,100 citations; 312 exhibits; and 321 source documents. The listed "sources" for this data include books from her personal library; the results of her library and correspondence research; a large number of photo-static copies of birth, death and marriage records; copies of county and state property tax and census records; and copies of military records. The people in her pedigree go back in history to the ancient Welsh kings, well beyond Rhys Goch, and their links to the Roman Empire; and to the Irish and Scottish royal house connections with Wales. They go back to the English kings beyond Edward III; to William the Conqueror; the French Emperor Charlemagne; and a second Roman Empire connection. Along the way are a variety of links to several other European countries. As with any genealogical work of this scope some errors may be present, but if there are any, they are most likely to concern peripheral individuals or events not particularly important to this pedigree.

At the back of this book is a "read only" CD that needs explanation for those who would use the data. There are several different programs on the CD in order to permit as wide an audience as possible. A detailed explanation is on page 40:

1. In order to accommodate individuals who use a computer program other than *The Master Genealogist*, a folder will be found on the CD that is entitled *"Data File. GED"*. This is a GEDCOM file using "Word-Pad" that will allow you to import the data to your own computer program. Also on the CD is a "Word" folder that contains this book, *"My Family Tree"*, and six *"family name folders"* that contain the document and picture images that are linked to this data.

2. For those individuals who are now using *The Master Genealogist, version 4.0d or version 5,* separate *"backup"* data for each will be found on the CD. This data needs only to be *"restored"* or *"imported"*, as appropriate, to your computer's TMG program. Persons with no computer program can easily access *"Second Site"*; the six *"family image folders"*; and the "Word" folder that contains this book directly from the CD.

There are a few established data-file ground rules that need to be reviewed at this time. Individuals may appear in one of five accent colors identifying the most important characteristic possessed by that individual. For instance, when a person's name is highlighted in *"yellow"*, that person is an *"ancestor"* (a grandmother, a grandfather, or a parent) – i.e.: a direct blood descendent. When a person's name is highlighted in *"red"*, that person is a *"relative"* (a cousin, an aunt, an uncle, a nephew, or a niece) – i.e.: an indirect blood relation. When a person's name is highlighted in *"green"*, that person is the original *"emigrant"* to this country of a particular family name. When a person is *"historically"* significant, the name is highlighted in *"brown"*. The fifth data-file color is a *"conflict"* color, and it appears as an *"aqua-blue"* color. It highlights an individual who falls into two or more of the above listed categories.

In the interest of more readily identifying the pedigree's *"ancestors"* and *"relatives"* in Europe, who are of particular interest to our study of the family tree, individuals who are *"titled"*, are of *"royalty"*, or who might normally be considered to be *"historically"* significant, are not flagged as *"historic"* persons. If this rule were not in effect, then those individuals would too frequently display the *"conflict"* color of two or more characteristics, and they would not be easily identifiable as an *"ancestor"* or a *"relative"*, which is our primary interest. However, if the individual was truly a *"historical"* person in Europe, such as King Edward I, William the Conqueror or Charlemagne, then that person is treated as an exception to the rule and is flagged *"historical"*. That person will then appear in the *"conflict"* color of *"aqua-blue"*. Generally, this is not a problem for individuals in America, so a different rule has been adopted. A person who was a Justice, Minister, Sheriff, Burgess, or a Councilor; or who served in the military; or who was a member of Congress; or who performed an act of historical significance, etc., is flagged as being *"historical"*, even though that person may also be an *"ancestor"* or a *"relative"*. Therefore, such a person in America appears in the *"conflict"* color of *"aqua-blue"*.

Several rules have been adopted to help determine reasonable *"tag event"* dates for individuals. First, if the date of birth of a parent's child is known and the name of the other parent is also known, then the date of marriage of the two parents is assumed to be *"about"* two years before the birth date of the oldest child. If the birth dates of the two parents are unknown, their birth dates are then assumed to be *"about"* twenty years before the assumed marriage date or the known marriage date. Second, the reverse of these assumptions is followed. If a person's birth date is known, then that person's marriage date is assumed to be *"about"* twenty years later if a spouse is known. Also, if the birth date of a child is unknown but the parent's marriage date is known, then the birth date of the oldest child is assumed to be *"about"* two years after the marriage. These rules and those of the preceding paragraph can be found in the TMG *"person view"* of Edward M. Moses under the "FILE-MEMO" buttons.

I have interspersed throughout the book a few screen prints of individuals from the *TMG 4.0d* program. The screens from *TMG 5* are somewhat different and include more data. In both versions of TMG, these screens may be either a *"person view"*, a *"family view"*, or a *"tree view"*. If the reader desires to examine a *"tag event"*, in order to find included *"memo"* details, *"citations"*, or *"source documents"* that relate to a particular person or event, then the reader should double-click on that person and follow the prompts in order to acquire that information.

There are a large number of scanned *"j.peg images"* that are accessible from the *"person view"* of those persons who have images (pictures or documents) in the data-file. To determine if a person has a document image in the data-file, look at the upper *"tool-bar"* for that person and identify the *"camera"* icon. If the camera icon is lighted and appears green, click on the camera icon. In TMG 4.0d, an index of all the scanned images for that person will appear on the screen. To view a particular image, highlight the one you would like to look at, and click on the *"Show Image"* button. A button for the zoom enlargement of the picture or document is readily visible. It is important that *TMG 4.0d* program be located in a *D-drive partition* on the hard drive, as all images are linked with D-drive partition paths to the individuals. This is not necessary for *TMG version 5* or for *Second Site*, where the linked images can be readily observed by anyone using the CD. The *TMG version 5* procedure to view an image is somewhat different from *version 4.d*, but is straightforward.

The following guidance is provided to facilitate using a TMG data-file. When the file is first opened, the *"person view"* of a person will appear on the screen. There are three possible views from left to right- *"Person"*, *"Family"*, and *"Tree"*. In order to open the screen to another person appearing in the same view, a double click on that person will accomplish that. In order to view an alphabetical listing of all persons in the data set, click on the *"binoculars"* icon on the tool bar. This is called the *"Pick List"*. Scroll to the desired person, highlight that person, and double click on that person to open the *"person view"*. From the *"person view"*, to open up a *"memo"*, click on the *"subject"* button. There may also be memos within the *"tag events"*. To view them, highlight the event and click on the *"edit"* button on the tool bar and select *"edit"*. To view a person's citation, highlight that citation. Click on the tool bar button *"citation"* and select *"edit"*. In order to view the *"source list"* and the source data, click on the tool bar button *"tools"*, and then click on the *"Master Source List"* button and follow the prompts.

The *"Second Site"* program by John Cardinal is also on the CD. It is there for individuals who have no computer genealogy program. To open that program, follow the following guidance:

1. Click on *"Second Site"* on the CD.
2. Click on the *"Second Site.exe"* icon
3. Click on the "File" button- then the "Open" button.
4. High-light *"Second Site.sdf"* - then click on "Open".
5. Click on the "File" button- and then on the "Browse" button. Navigate.

This *"Second Site"* program provides narratives and images on the individuals in the data-file.

TMG users may access two *preset* reports in the *"Report Menu"* of *TMG 4d and TMG 5* to generate either an *"Individual Narrative"* or *"Individual Detail"* report for any selected individual. With the selected individual in the *"person view"*, click on the "Reports" tab on the tool-bar. At the bottom of the reports menu select the desired report (1 or 2).

MY FAMILY TREE

TABLE OF CONTENTS

Dedication: 3
Introduction: 4-7
Table of Contents: 8

Chapter 1:   The Early Years and a Developing Interest in Genealogy 9-18

Chapter 2:   A Henderson – Lewis Marriage ………………………........ 19-23

Chapter 3:   A Paternal Line to the Emigrant John Lewis 24-25

Chapter 4:   Back Into Ancient Wales ………………………………....... 26-28

Chapter 5:   A Maternal Line to the Emigrant John Lewis ……………........... 29

Chapter 6:   A Connection to the Washington Family 30

Chapter 7:   The Dymoke and Gascoigne Families 31-32

Chapter 8:   Pedigree Branches into Ireland, Scotland, and France 33-34

Chapter 9:   "Tree Limbs" With Historical Persons in America 35-36

Chapter 10: The Moses Genealogical Record 37-38

Chapter 11: A Summary of this Pedigree's Odyssey 39

CHAPTER ONE

THE EARLY YEARS AND A DEVELOPING INTEREST IN GENEALOGY

On November 11, 1908, **Grace May McLean (Moses) (1908-1996)** was born in her grandfather's house on 714 Highland Avenue in Norfolk, Virginia. Her mother was **Agnes May Hanley (1890-1985)**, whose family had its roots in Gloucester County in Tidewater, Virginia, north of Norfolk. Agnes was born at Sarah's Creek in Gloucester County on April 1, 1890. Her mother was **Margaret "Maggie" Sarah Henderson (1856-1902)** and her father was **James Hanley (1846-1917)**. Grace's father was **Frederick Leland McLean (1886-1913)**. He was the great grandson of **Lauchlin McLean (c1786-1855)**, a Scottish immigrant who settled on Jannin's Island in Arichat, Nova Scotia, Canada. While it is known that he was an emigrant from Scotland, his ancestry within that country and the McLean clan has not been traced further. Grace's McLean grandfather was **William McLean, Jr. (1846-1910),** whose father in turn was **William McLean, Sr. (1820-a1860),** who immigrated to Norfolk from Laughlin McLean's home in Nova Scotia.

Agnes and Frederick Leland McLean were married on September 10, 1907, in Elizabeth City, NC. They had two children, Grace and her younger brother **Frederick Leland McLean, Jr. (1911-1974)**. There was no written family history at the time of Grace's birth, and there were no family records of note relating to the family's genealogy. However, as Grace grew into maturity her mother Agnes would relate the family's oral history with stories that she remembered from her own early childhood while growing up in Gloucester County. These stories instilled in Grace an awareness of her family being connected to some well-known and historical "Tidewater" families. A few of the family names that were imbedded in Grace's childhood memory included Lewis, Warner, Henderson, Lee, Custis, Washington, Spann, and Tilney. At the time, these names meant little to the young girl growing up in Norfolk. Later however, they would have great meaning as she began to research her family roots.

Grace's early childhood in Norfolk was not easy. Her father, Frederick Leland McLean, was a telephone company employee who disappeared suddenly while on a business trip to New Jersey. Foul play was immediately suspected, because his disappearance occurred during a period of violent northern union organizing and labor riots. I hold a wonderful letter that he wrote while on this trip to New Jersey in which he expresses his desire to return soon to his family in Norfolk, but that was not to be. His family's efforts to locate him were fruitless, and on April 26, 1918, the Court of Hustings in Portsmouth, VA, declared him legally dead. Life was very hard for the small family of the widow and her two small children. They lived for a time with her husband's McLean relatives in Norfolk, a common practice in that time. Some of the Hanley family members also lived in Norfolk, and they too helped provide some support. Agnes did "piece-work" to provide funds, a measure of the young family's poor financial condition. Another measure of scant means was that Grace did not have a Christmas tree in her home until she was twelve years old. The family was typically Christian and god-fearing, yet Grace was not baptized until April 6, 1924, when she was fifteen years old and was living in greatly improved conditions in Washington, DC, with a wonderful step-father. She was confirmed an Episcopalian in St. Paul's Episcopal Church in Rock Creek Parish on the same day that she was baptized. Agnes and both of her children, Grace and Frederick, Jr., had survived extremely tough times in Norfolk, but with the help of an important person who was about to enter their lives, a new chapter in their life was about to begin.

In 1917, a Marine sergeant, **John Edward Mason (1861-1940)**, who was then stationed in Norfolk, met Agnes and her two children. He was a remarkable man in many ways and I still remember him with great love and respect. He was fifty-six years old and had never been married. He grew up in Yorkville, SC, a town now named York. When the "Yankees" entered Yorkville, during the War Between the States the young boy hid under his bed, a beautiful hand made oak four poster double bed that is now in my possession. After the war, as a young boy during the terrible post-war period called "Reconstruction", an era of much lawlessness and disorder throughout the south, he rode as a courier for the former confederate general Wade Hampton, an important leader and organizer of South Carolina's Ku Klux Klan. At that time the Klan offered most of the security and protection available to law-abiding citizens in the state. Wade Hampton was later elected governor of the state and served in the U.S. Congress. John Edward Mason had always wanted to be a soldier and he wanted very much to enter the United States Military Academy at West Point, NY, but in the still angry post-war climate, his father forbade it. Instead, he went to Davidson College in NC, a fine Presbyterian institution. He became fluent in four languages, including Greek, Latin, and German. He also studied the law and history. After graduation, he practiced law and taught school for a time, before finally deciding to follow his first love, the military. He enlisted in the U.S. cavalry and was posted in the west where he fought Apache Indians, including the Apache Geronimo, known as "The Power". Years later he left the cavalry and entered the U.S. Marine Corps, serving with the Marines during both the Spanish-American War and World War I. As he was nearing retirement from the Marines, John Edward Mason met and began to court the widow Agnes Hanley McLean in Norfolk.

The Marines had reassigned Operations Sergeant Mason to Washington, DC, for his final tour of duty when he proposed marriage to Agnes in Norfolk; a proposal she accepted. They were married on 1 June, 1918, and Agnes' family moved north to Washington to join him. Grace's life now changed dramatically. Later in her life, she would often credit John Edward Mason and her future husband Merillat Moses, as the two men in her life with the most influence on her mental and character development. Her mother's early relating of the family's oral history and John Mason's extensive knowledge of history, as well as his stressing of the overall importance of education, all came together at this point in her life to encourage a lifelong respect and love of history. She became an excellent student and began to develop the remarkable powers of memory that in later life would astonish both her family and friends. Mr. Mason also inspired the development of a high degree of personal character and morality in his stepdaughter

Grace. In the future, it would be difficult for Grace to accept "shades of gray", when she felt that she knew what was really "right". This trait stood her in good stead in her future genealogical work, which she always approached with thoroughness, dedication, and honesty. John Mason's own great intellect, honesty, and knowledge played a major role in shaping Grace's character, and in training her mind to be highly critical and rational. She used to say that on "issues" she felt that she thought more like a man, rational and unemotional. I can still remember sitting on the living room floor next to Mr. Mason's lounge chair as he smoked his pipe, or sitting with him at the kitchen table at night, drinking warm milk and eating soda crackers, as he held my attention with many interesting stories. He was a real teacher and a gentleman. His high standing in the family is best attested to by his family nickname "Daddy Mason". Agnes had chosen well.

Grace matriculated to Central High School in Washington in 1922. It was here that she met the second man who was to impact her life greatly, my father **Merillat Moses (1909-1988)**, who was her classmate at Central High, arguably one of the best schools in the country at that time. Both families lived in the Petworth district of Washington, DC, near Rock Creek Cemetery and the Old Soldier's Home. Grace's family lived at 4021 Marlboro Place in DC. Merillat, whose nickname was "Mickey", lived nearby on Quincy Street. His mother, **Edna Richardson Merillat (1884-1964)**, was a fourth generation Washingtonian. Her Merillat ancestors were Swiss French Huguenots. Mickey's father, **LeRoy Hiram Moses (1878-1959)**, was born in Cambridge Springs, PA, where his father was the publisher of the local newspaper. "Roy" was a descendent of the shipwright **Emigrant John Moses (c1610-a1661) of Plymouth and Duxbury, MA**, an emigrant from Wales. John Moses' family had their own family coat-of-arms in Wales, "*three cocks and a chevron*", which had been awarded by the English king. Coincidentally, Grace discovered on a trip to Wales that John Moses came from the same Welsh county, Monmouthshire, as her own Virginia ancestor **John Lewis (1592-1657)**. But that is getting ahead of the story. The Moses family is believed to have two Mayflower lines through marriage (Mary Brown and Alden Pond), which I have not yet confirmed. Roy Moses was employed in the Civil Service in the Navy Department for forty-four years and rose to be the second ranking civil service employee during World War II. He managed the navy wartime budget and testified frequently before Congress on budgetary matters. His work for the navy was so valued by the navy's admirals that they permitted him to receive his personal medical care at the Naval Hospital in Bethesda.

Both of my parents were superior students and they graduated from Central High School in 1926. They had dated through high school, and Mickey frequently serenaded Grace on her family's front porch while playing a mandolin. He had a natural instinct for playing musical instruments (mandolin, piano, violin, and the accordion) throughout his life. He never received formal instruction, always playing by ear. Grace matriculated to George Washington University and received a BA Cum-Laude with Distinction in 1930, with majors in English and History. She always took advantage of every opportunity in her course work to acquire more knowledge in her first academic love, history. She was on the women's national championship rifle team and was active in her Phi Beta Kappa sorority. During her last two years, family finances required that she attend night school in order to complete her degree requirements, while still working at the U.S. State

Department. At Central High School, Mickey was a ROTC cadet with the rank of Lieutenant and was a distance runner on the track team. In 1926, he attended a special prep school, in order to prepare for a competitive exam for an appointment to the United States Military Academy at West Point, NY. He won the appointment of the Vice President of the United States and entered the academy in July of 1927, graduating four years later. While at the academy, Mickey was a long distance track runner, sang in the cadet chapel choir, developed an excellent proficiency at poker, and was a Cadet Lieutenant in his First Class (senior) year. Grace frequently visited Mickey at West Point to attend dances during his four years at the academy. Several persons have told me over the years that the cadet hostess at West Point was quoted as having said that Grace was the prettiest girl she had ever seen visiting at West Point. During Mickey's First Class year at the Military Academy, Grace had graduated from George Washington University, but she continued to work at the State Department in order to save a small marriage "dowry". The couple planned to marry soon after Mickey's graduation and his commissioning in the army as a Second Lieutenant.

During the summer of 1931, Grace and Mickey, now a newly commissioned second lieutenant in the horse-dawn field artillery, eloped to Portsmouth, Virginia. The couple married on a Saturday afternoon, August 22nd, at St. John's Episcopal Church where Rector William A. Brown officiated. They then returned to Washington, DC, where they spent a brief time with Mickey's parents before driving to Fort Bragg, NC, his first army duty station. They and two other newly married couples from West Point were welcomed to the post with a horse drawn "caisson ride", memorialized in a wonderful old photograph. Grace adapted quickly to life as an army officer's wife. Frequent entertaining and "social calls" in the evenings at the homes of other officers were expected in the "old army" of the 1930's. Their initial home was a converted World War I frame hospital barracks, which challenged Grace's home decorating skills. Their first living room sofa was an army cot covered by Grace and their first cooking stove was wood burning. In those days the artillery was horse-drawn, and Mickey purchased the required officer's horse. Grace took riding lessons, and Mickey was a regular on the golf course on Wednesday and Saturday afternoons. Grace had little prior experience cooking and I recall her story of the first dinner she prepared for guests, when she started a fire in the stove by placing the bread, still wrapped in paper, into the stove. Mickey would often tell the story of how they produced home-made whiskey during the era of prohibition by first cooking it, then placing it in a barrel container on the back of a rocking chair, and rocking on the front porch of their quarters in the evenings. In spite of not having many material things, I know that they enjoyed those times and looked back on them with great fondness.

The days, months, and years passed quickly. Grace bore two sons, the first at Ft. Bragg and the second at Ft. Sill. She named her first son, this book's author, **Edward Merillat (born on June 26, 1932)**, after both her stepfather and Mickey's mother's family, a measure of the high esteem she held for "Daddy Mason". She named her second son **Charles Custis (born on April, 30, 1936)**, the name Custis being in her family's oral history. Between these two sons was one miscarriage. During the ensuing years we lived twice at Ft. Bragg and twice at Ft. Sill, OK. In between those moves, we lived in a

Philadelphia suburb for a year in 1937, while Mickey studied for a Masters Degree in physics at the University of Pennsylvania. The family finances were very tight at that time while not living on an army post, and Grace baked lots of bread weekly to save a little money. The family was in its second tour at Ft. Sill from 1939 to 1941, when John Edward Mason passed away in his sleep on 11 January, 1940, in Washington, DC, while trying to recover from a severe cold. Grace went east for his funeral, and he was interred in Rosehill Cemetery, York, SC. A year later on December 7, 1941, while the family was attending a Sunday matinee movie in the Ft. Sill Post Theater, the film was suddenly stopped. An officer quickly mounted the stage and announced that the Japanese had just attacked Pearl Harbor and that all military personnel were ordered immediately to their duty posts. We went home to speculate on the effect that this news would have on our lives. Soon thereafter, Mickey was ordered to the West Coast to help organize and train a field artillery observation battalion as its executive officer.

Grace decided to return to Washington with her two sons in order to be close to hers and Mickey's parents, during what was expected to be a long war with Japan and Germany. My grandfather Roy drove out to Ft. Sill to help with the move and to drive the family back east to Washington. Grace was soon looking for a family home in the Washington area. She wanted to purchase a house, but she had very little cash saved from an army officer's salary. Mickey was only a captain when the war started. She managed to scrape together the necessary down payment, however, mostly by taking loans on family life insurance policies. She bought her first house at 7624 Bradley Boulevard in Bethesda, MD, located behind the private Landon School for boys. It was to be the first of several house purchases over the years, all of them profitable. This new house was in an excellent location, and the Bradley Elementary School was within an easy bicycle ride. I attended this school in the fifth and sixth grades and my brother Charlie attended through the fifth grade. Buying this house was a tight financial squeeze for the family, and wartime rationing was in effect. Charlie and I shared maintenance tasks for the half-acre lawn and had several miscellaneous weekly chores. I built a doghouse for "Lochinvar", our hound dog, and "Thomas Jefferson Cat" tried to stay out of trouble. Grandmother Agnes Mason was living alone at this time in Washington, because her son Frederick McLean Jr., Grace's brother, had entered the Marine Corps. So Grace invited her to live with the family in our new home in Bethesda. For several months she spent considerable time and effort assisting Agnes in preparing for the Civil Service exam so that she could become a civil service employee. She passed the exam and joined the Veterans Administration, ultimately becoming a supervisor and finally retiring with a much needed pension.

In 1943, Mickey returned from California to rejoin the family. He was assigned to the army staff to work in intelligence in the newly constructed Pentagon located in Washington, DC. He had a top-secret assignment with the military intelligence staff; he was tasked to devise ways to counter the German V-1 and V-2 rocket missile attacks on Britain. His graduate degree in physics was probably the reason for his selection for this job. The family was finally together again, but his hours at the Pentagon were long and unpredictable, and raising the family was still Grace's show. She gave birth to her third son, **John Warner Lewis (born on November 11, 1944)** at the Naval Hospital in

Bethesda. It is quite clear from the names she gave to each of her sons that she was thinking about the family's genealogy, but she was not yet actively pursuing the family history. However, she had undoubtedly absorbed more oral history from her mother while Agnes was living with our family in Bethesda. I graduated from Bradley Elementary School in 1944 and enrolled in Gordon Junior High School in Washington, where the school system at that time was superior to the schools in Montgomery County, MD. I attended Gordon in the seventh and eighth grades while World War II was raging. Each day I traveled into Washington with a car pool to the "district line", a trip Grace had arranged with some government employees. This was a period of strict gas rationing. The travel to school finished with a long trolley car ride from the "district line" down Wisconsin Avenue and into Georgetown where Gordon was located. During those summers in Bethesda, the family planted and tended a "Victory Garden" in a vacant field on the other side of Bradley Boulevard, where we raised lettuce, potatoes, carrots, radishes, tomatoes, and corn. In that same large and empty field I played pickup baseball almost daily with other neighborhood boys.

As 1945 came to a close, Mickey was ordered to Frankfurt, Germany, to serve with the "Army of Occupation". His new job in Germany was still counter-intelligence. We were to join him there six months later in the summer of 1946. In June of 1946, Grace and her three sons packed up for the move to Germany. John was still a baby of one and one-half years. She sold the Bethesda house. We boarded a military transport ship, the USS Holbrook, at Ft. Hamilton, NJ, and sailed to Bremerhaven, Germany, where we debarked at night after ten seasick days. We were all tired and hungry and immediately boarded a military night train to Frankfurt, where Mickey met us and drove us to our new home in an army vehicle. While Mickey was in Germany, Grace had realized a significant profit on the sale of the Bethesda house. She spent some of this profit on an order placed with Galt's jewelry store in Washington to manufacture three gold "family crest" rings, one for each of her three sons. Each ring bore an engraved *"Welsh dragon with a bloody 'red hand' in its mouth" and the words "Omni Solum Forti Patria Est" (Every Land is Home to the Brave).* The story behind this engraving, related to us at the time by Grace, was that of two brothers who were challenged by their father to establish their right to a newly discovered land. The first to touch this land could claim it. One brother, falling behind in the boat race, severed his hand and threw it to the shore, winning the new land. This story is not now believed to be factual, but the "crest" is very real. It is in fact the arms of **Rhys Goch, Lord of Ystrad-yw & Ewyas (c960-a 990)**, an ancient king who was descended from all six of the "Royal Tribes of Wales", and who Grace later proved to be one of our family's great grandfathers. These "arms" were also found on the tombstone of the Emigrant John Lewis of Gloucester. It's quite clear that while she had not yet dedicated herself to actively researching the family genealogy at the age of thirty-eight, she was making a strong statement by purchasing these three very expensive rings; it was a purchase inspired by Agnes' oral family history.

In Frankfurt the family lived in a very nice confiscated house in the fenced and secured American compound. A few houses on our street and also behind our street had been heavily bombed, and we could occasionally smell odors of decomposition. We had a maid, a cook, a nursemaid, and a gardener. Mickey's job was again classified, but he later revealed that he had played a role in a major counter-intelligence effort that targeted soviet agents in the American Zone of West Germany by utilizing former German army intelligence personnel. He also participated in the recruitment of Werner Von Braun and other German rocket and missile scientists, and helped to secretly relocate them to the United States. Once there, they became the foundation for the organization of the National Aeronautics and Space Agency (NASA) and America's space and missile program. The military government had established a Barter-Mart store to reduce black-market activities and to facilitate the mutually agreeable and fair exchange of such items as food, cigarettes, sugar, and chocolate for German furniture, crystal, silver, jewelry, cameras, and artwork. Grace used this period in her life to acquire many beautiful and valuable pieces for her future homes. She had oil portraits of each member of the family painted by a well-known German artist. She developed a life-long fondness for the German longhaired dachshund, which was relatively unknown in America. When she returned to America in 1949, she brought back male and female dogs named "Cito" and "Dorie". Their pups later founded a kennel in McLean, Virginia. For the rest of her life she would always have a longhaired dachshund. In Germany Charlie and I attended American schools that were established for American dependent children. I was in the ninth grade and Charlie was in the sixth. However, it was soon apparent that the high school was not good enough to prepare me for winning an appointment to the Military Academy, which is where I wanted to go to college. So after my freshman year, I returned alone to America by troop transport ship and entered a private school on an athletic scholarship, the St. James School in Hagerstown, MD. I attended St. James in my sophomore and junior years, played varsity baseball, soccer, and football, and was ranked second academically in my class. The family relocated to Heidelberg shortly after I left Germany, which is where Mickey completed the last half of his duty tour before returning to the United States.

Upon their return the family lived in Norfolk, where Mickey attended the Armed Forces Staff College. He was subsequently assigned to the Joint Chiefs of Staff in the Pentagon. Grace purchased her second home, located in Sumner, MD, and I skipped the senior year of high school at St. James in order to attend the Hilder School in 1949 in Washington. This special prep school prepared its students for the highly competitive entrance exams to the Military Academy and to the Naval Academy. In July 1950, there would be a larger number than usual of presidential appointments to West Point (75), which meant a better chance to secure an appointment. It was a very intense year of study, but I placed forty-fourth in the country for West Point and fifth for Annapolis, winning an appointment to both academies. During the year, Grace had begun writing to Congressman Bland from the 1st District of Virginia (Gloucester and Tidewater). Using old family names from the oral history she had learned from her mother Agnes, she convinced Congressman Bland, who was about to retire, to award his annual principal appointment to West Point to me. Now having a congressional appointment, I gave up the presidential appointment and entered the academy from the 1st District of Virginia on July 4, 1950. The Korean War had started a week earlier. While at the Academy, I participated in several cadet activities, including the cadet chapel choir for three years. I was the running back on the brigade football championship team in 1951, and spent two years on the cheerleading squad. My First Class year, I was the Head Cheerleader and served as a Cadet Lieutenant.

The family remained in the Washington area for two more years, when Mickey received orders to be the new Army Military Attaché to Uruguay and Paraguay. The family went first to the Army Language School at the Presidio of Monterey, where both Grace and Mickey studied Spanish for six months, before sailing on the USS United States to Montevideo, Uruguay. Charlie entered West Point with a Presidential Appointment in the summer of 1953 and the Korean War ended as I graduated from the Military Academy on June 4, 1954. I selected the armor branch based on my class standing and was ordered to report to Ft. Knox, KY, in late August for the Basic Armor Course. The family was still living in Uruguay and had missed my graduation from the Academy. But Mickey's 1931 classmates presented me with a Colt .32 caliber pistol as a graduation present. While enroute to my first duty assignment at Ft. Knox in August, I drove Grandmother Agnes to York, SC, so she could attend the funeral of "Daddy Mason's" sister, Aunt **Bessie Meek Mason (1865-1954)**. Following basic armor training at Ft. Knox, I completed airborne training at Ft. Benning, GA, and then ranger school, before reporting to Ft. Bragg, NC, for duty with the 82d Airborne Division. The family returned to the Washington area in 1955 from Uruguay and Grace purchased her third home, a fine colonial house in Arlington County at 1129 North Ivanhoe Street. With two sons away from home and Mickey's army career beginning to wind down (he retired in 1960), Grace was now ready to devote a lot of her time and energies to her long delayed research project, determining her family's genealogical history. For the next forty years she sought the derivation of her pedigree with an unmatched passion and devotion. Only the loss of her eyesight through macular degeneration in 1988 and Mickey's passing away that same year slowed her down in the 1990's. Even after that, her mind remained sharp and her incredible memory continued to amaze people with detailed family historical and genealogical information.

So in the late 1950's Grace finally began her second career, her first having been that of an army officer's wife. Mickey would frequently drive her into Washington, where she would spend the day at the Library of Congress, or the National Archives. She joined many genealogical and historical organizations and spent many hours in the Daughters of the Revolution (DAR) library. In her search for her family pedigree, she determined to first explore the several families that had been revealed to her through Agnes's oral family stories. This led her to begin an investigation of the Henderson and Lewis families. She knew from Agnes that a great grandmother was a Lewis and that a great grandfather was a Henderson. She also knew that the Lewises were a well known and highly respected family that had owned and lived for many years at Warner Hall. So this is how Grace's great odyssey began. She would finally conclude her search forty years later, a search that revealed a truly remarkable family tree and roots. We shall follow several of its branches back into Wales, England, Scotland, Ireland, and France, starting with Chapter 2 and the important Henderson-Lewis connection.

"TREE VIEW" OF
GRACE McLEAN MOSES

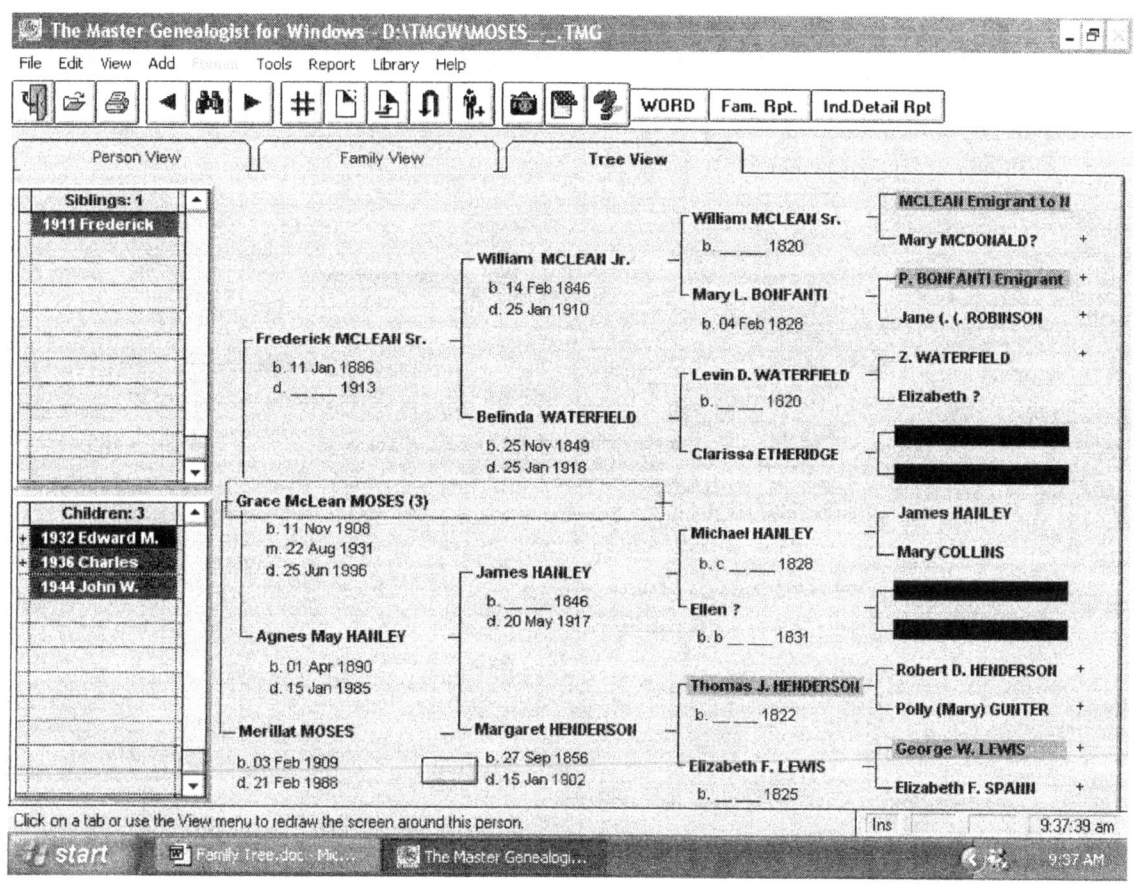

"PERSON VIEW" OF

AGNES MAY HANLEY

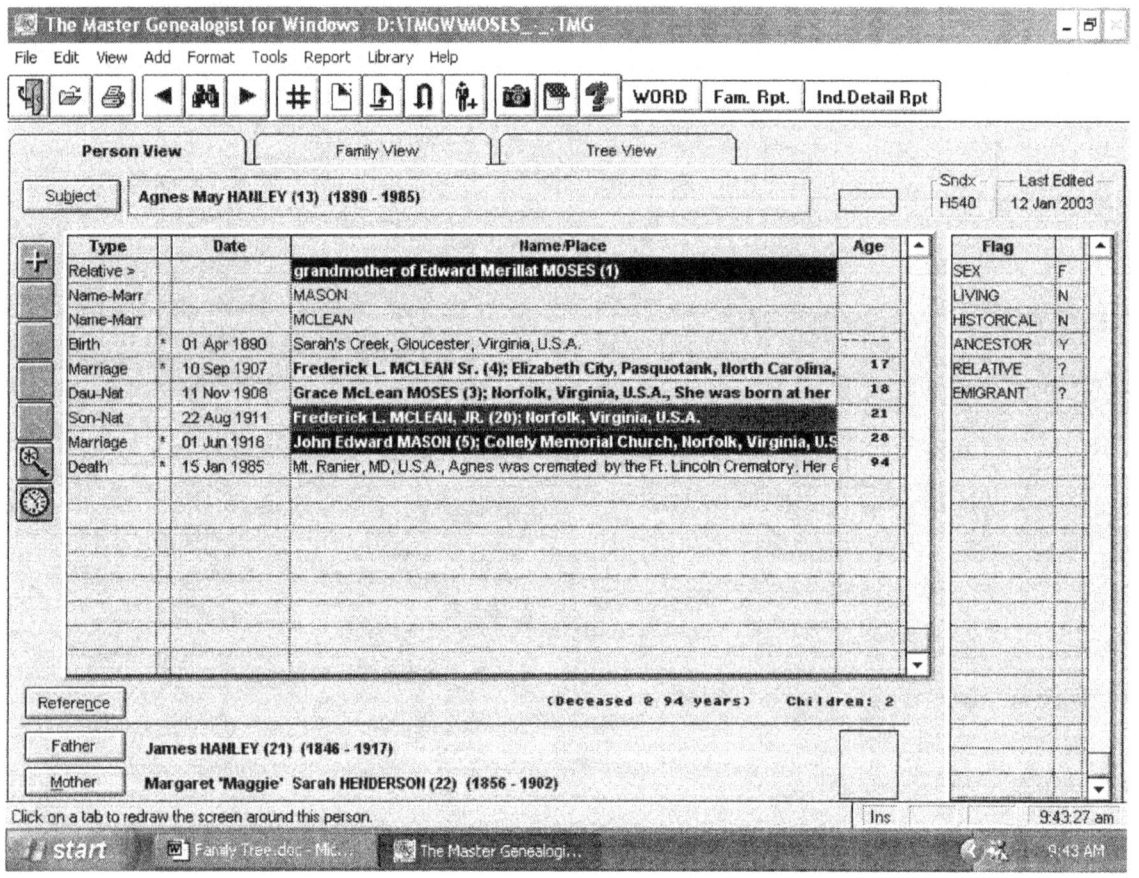

CHAPTER TWO

A HENDERSON – LEWIS MARRIAGE

Agnes' mother **Margaret "Maggie" Sarah Henderson (1856-1902)** was born in Gloucester County, VA. Maggie married **James Hanley (1846-1917)** on 13 November 1875. She died in Norfolk at the age of fifty-four. James Hanley was born in Baltimore, MD and died in Pykesville, MD. His occupational trade was recorded as "fisherman". He enlisted for "three years or the duration of the war" in the Confederate Army during the War Between the States, where he served in Company G and E of the 2d Maryland Regiment. James Hanley received severe wounds at Davis Farm in the "Battle of Weldon Railroad" and was released from the Springfield Hospital in 1864. Agnes was one of seven children, four sons and three daughters, born to Margaret and James Hanley.

Agnes' grandparents included **Thomas Jefferson Henderson (1822-1861)** and **Elizabeth Frances Lewis (1825-1896)**. Thomas Jefferson Henderson, Grace's great grandfather, was a "mariner" and he was thought to be a Chesapeake Bay "pilot". He owned the schooner *Mary Anne,* which was hired by the Confederate States of America during the War Between the States. Thomas Henderson was a descendent of **Governor George Yeardley (1580-1627),** Grace's eleventh great grandfather. George Yeardley was an ancestor of the Custis, Thorougood, Littleton, and Harmonson families of Virginia. He was an emigrant to the Virginia Colony in 1609 and was knighted by the King of England. George Yeardley was appointed Governor of the Colony in 1608 and summoned the first legislative assembly ever convened in America. During the War Between the States, Thomas Jefferson Henderson, who was of Scotch descent, served with the "*Gloucester Invincibles"* in Company F, 26th Regiment of Virginia Infantry, in the Confederate Army. He died of "swamp fever" while in the army, and his name is inscribed on the Confederate Monument that is located outside the Gloucester County Courthouse. There are eight generations of Henderson ancestors listed in this pedigree CD, beginning with Thomas Jefferson Henderson and ending with **James Henderson, the Emigrant (1641-1722).**

Elizabeth Frances Lewis (1825-1896) was Grace's great grandmother. She was born in 1825 at Sarah's Creek in Gloucester County. In 1844 she married Thomas Jefferson Henderson and they had six children, four sons and two daughters, one of whom was Grace's grandmother, Margaret "Maggie" Sarah Henderson. Maggie's mother was Elizabeth Frances Lewis, Grace's first proven connection to the **Emigrant John Lewis (1592-1657)**. Later, Grace was able to prove a second line to the Emigrant. The first line went to **John Lewis III of Warner Hall (1669-1725)**, "*the Councilor*", and the second line went to John's brother **Captain Edward Lewis (1667-1713)**. Both were sons of **Major/Colonel John Lewis, Jr. (1633-1690)**, who in turn was the son of the Emigrant John Lewis. It should be pointed out at this time that the wife of John Lewis III, "*the Councilor*" of Warner Hall, was **Elizabeth Warner (1672-1720)**. Their marriage brought the large and powerful Warner Hall plantation holdings into the Lewis family and firmly established the political and economic importance of the Lewis family in Virginia.

Elizabeth Warner was a descendent of **George Reade, the Emigrant (1608-1674)**, whose mother, **Mildred Windebank, (c1587-1630)**, descended from the famous **Windebank, Dymoke, and Gascoigne** families of English nobility. These contributions to our pedigree will be covered in a later chapter.

Elizabeth Warner's parents were **Colonel Augustine Warner Jr. (II) (1642-1681)** and **Mildred Reade (1642-1694)**. He was known as *"the Speaker"* of the House of Burgesses. His father was the **Emigrant Colonel Augustine Warner Sr. (1610-1674**, who built and lived at Warner Hall, patented in 1642. He was a Burgess, Justice, and a member of the Council from Gloucester County in 1651-1658. After Elizabeth, there are six generations of the Warner family on the CD back to **William Warner (c1495-c1529)**. Elizabeth Warner's mother Mildred has an impressive pedigree derived from her father the **Emigrant George Reade (1608-1674),** who descended from sixteen Magna Charta Sureties and King Edward III of England. He is our family's primary *"Magna Charta"* link and the *"Daughters of the Barons of Runnemede"* ancestral link going back to **Saier De Quincy (c1088-a1110)** of Buckley and Daventry England, whose son **Lord Robert De Quincy (c1110-c1198)** was a Crusader. Saier De Quincy was Grace's twenty-fourth great grandfather. Emigrant George Reade, Elizabeth Warner's ancestor, came to Virginia in 1637 with Governor Harvey. He was a member of the Council, Acting Secretary of State from 1637-1641, Acting Governor of Virginia in 1638, and a Burgess for James City 1649-1656. The CD carries the Reade family back four generations from the Emigrant George Reade to **Richard Reade (c1473-1555)**.

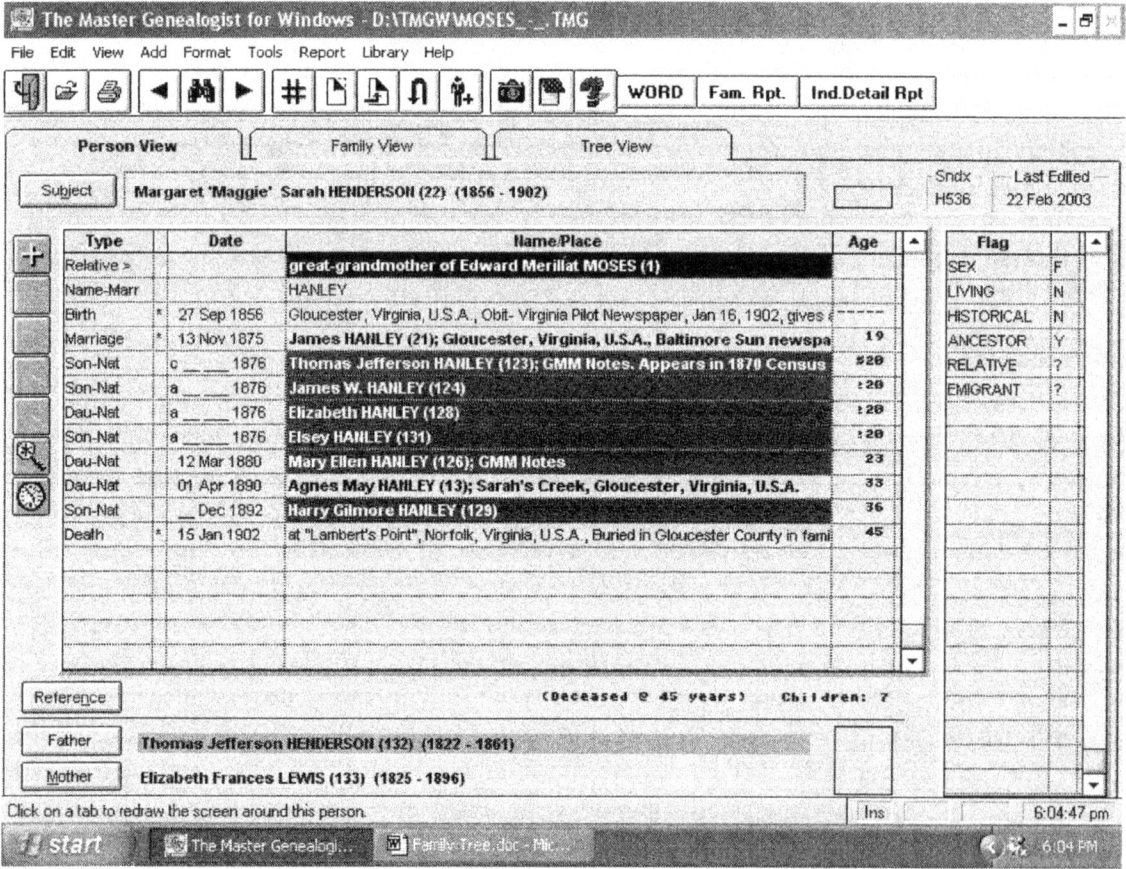

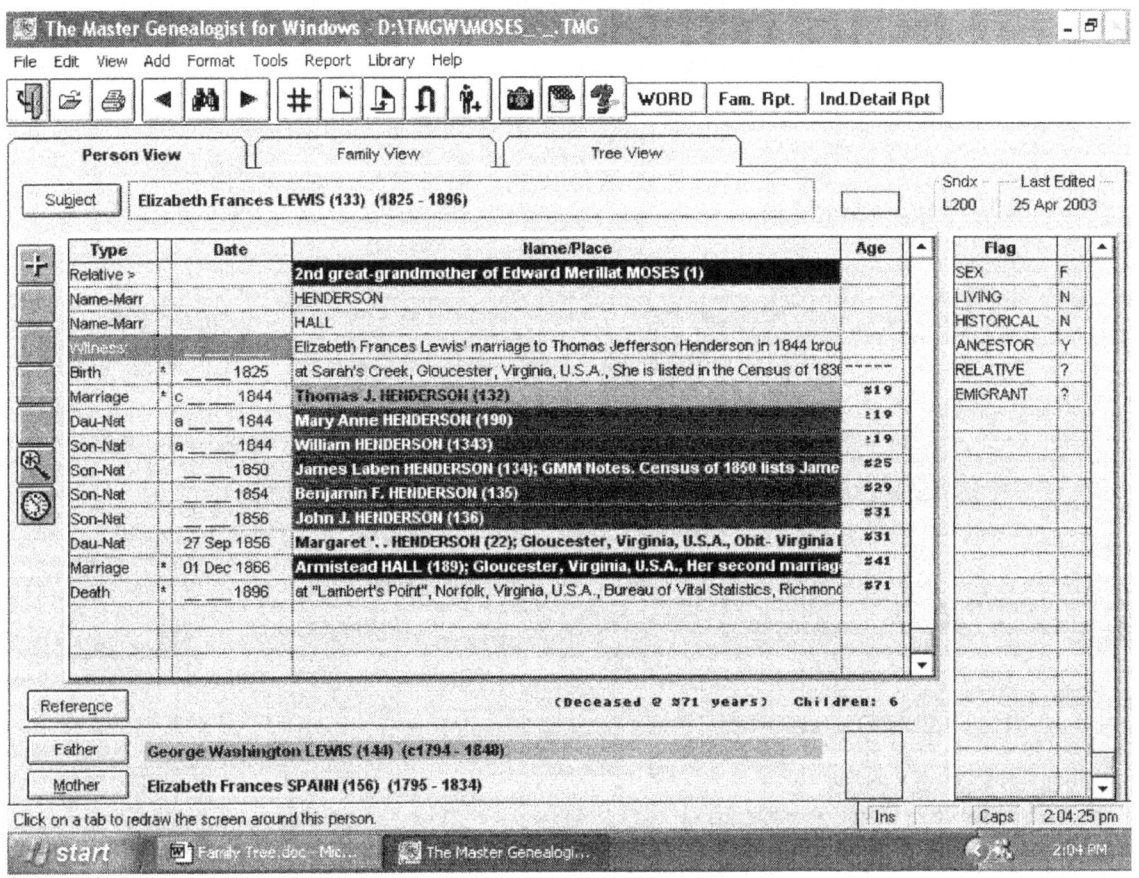

Elizabeth Frances Lewis' parents were **George Washington Lewis (c1794-1848) and Elizabeth Frances Spann (1795-1834)**. Grace's research proved that George Washington Lewis was her second great grandfather, and that he was the connection for a double ancestral line going back to the Emigrant John Lewis through two of the Emigrant's grandsons, Captain Edward Lewis and his brother, "*Councilor*" John Lewis III of Warner Hall. George Washington Lewis is listed in the Gloucester 1810 Personal Property Tax List and the 1820 Gloucester Census. One of his ancestral lines to the Emigrant is from his mother **Mary Whiting Hubard (c1776-1830),** to his grandmother Mary Whiting, to John Whiting, and then to Mary Skaife, Ann Lewis, Captain Edward Lewis, Maj./Col. John Lewis, Jr., and finally to the Emigrant John Lewis. The second ancestral line is from his father, **John Lewis of Mathews County (c1770-1809)** back through three generations of John Lewis', to the "*Councilor*" John Lewis III of Warner Hall, to Maj./Col. John Lewis Jr. and to the Emigrant John Lewis.

George Washington Lewis was retained by Fielding Lewis to manage "Belle Farm" for Thomas Lewis's family from 1810-1820. Thomas had inherited the farm, an original part of the Warner Hall estate, from his father Col. Warner Lewis, III Esq. of Warner Hall. When Thomas died in 1805, Fielding Lewis then inherited "Belle Farm", because Thomas Lewis and his wife Anne Lewis had produced no children. Fielding Lewis had initially hired **John Lewis of Mathews County (c1770-1809)**, Thomas's cousin, to manage "Belle Farm", which he did until his death in 1809. Fielding Lewis then retained George Washington Lewis, who managed the farm until 1820. In 1812 George Washington Lewis married **Elizabeth Frances Spann (1795-1834)** of Gloucester County. This marriage appears in the 1833 Gloucester Land Book. The couple produced two sons and two daughters. One of their daughters was Grace's great grandmother, Elizabeth Frances Lewis.

"PERSON VIEW" OF

GEORGE WASHINGTON LEWIS

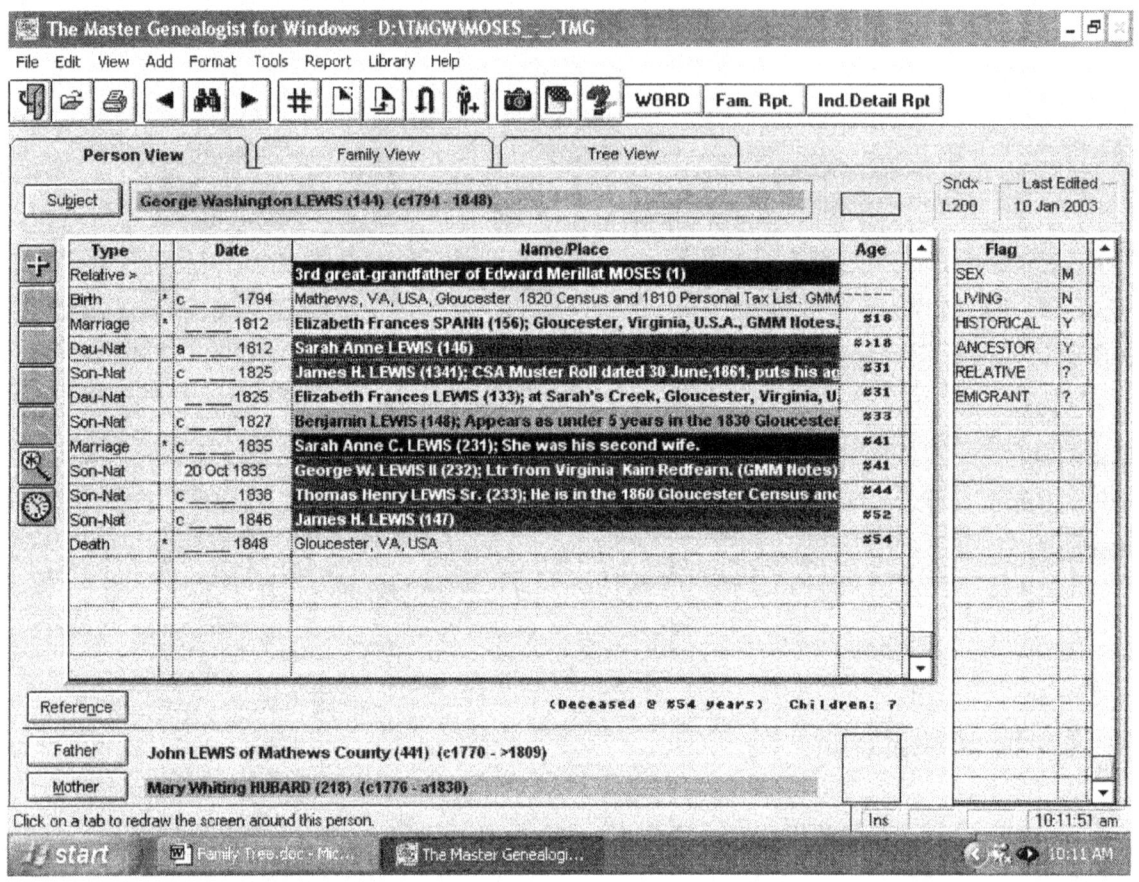

"TREE VIEW" OF

COLONEL JOHN LEWIS IV OF WARNER HALL

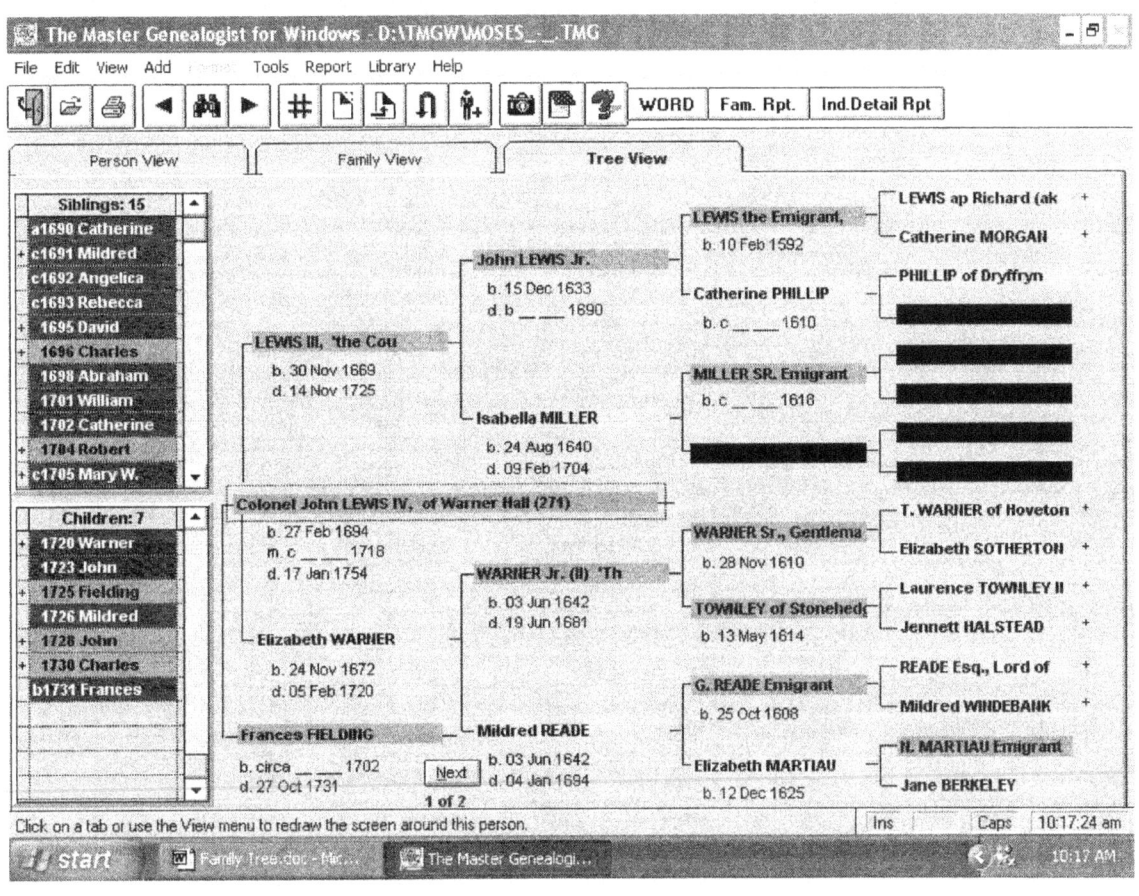

CHAPTER THREE

A PATERNAL LINE TO JOHN LEWIS THE EMIGRANT

John Lewis of Mathews County (c1770-c1809) was the father of George Washington Lewis, Grace's third great grandfather. He was born in Mathews County, which separated from Gloucester County in 1791, and he lived at *"Milford Haven"* in Mathews County. The 1802 Gloucester Taxable Property List identifies him as *"John Lewis (C)"*, i.e. *"son of Christopher"*. His brother Christopher Todd Lewis, Jr. is listed in this same manner in the 1801 and 1802 Mathews County Taxable Property Lists. The 1803-1807 and 1809 Personal Property Tax lists of Gloucester County list John Lewis as *"John Lewis of Abingdon"*. The man named *"Christopher"* in the tax list is **Christopher Todd Lewis (1749-c1800).** He is the father of our John Lewis of Mathews County and his birth appears in the *"Kingston Parish Register"*. In 1792, John Lewis of Mathews County married **Mary Whiting Hubard (1776-a1830)** and they had two sons. One of these sons was our George Washington Lewis, whose parents provide us with a double connection to the Emigrant John Lewis.

Christopher Todd Lewis' mother was **Lucretia Booth (c1737-a1782)** of Kingston Parish in Gloucester County, Grace's fifth great grandmother. Through Lucretia Booth Grace is related to the Booth, Armistead, Lee, Mason, and Cooke families of Virginia. In 1766, Christopher Todd Lewis' marriage to **Catherine "Caty" Peed (c1750-1809)** is recorded in the *"Kingston Parish Register"*. They had five children, one of whom was our John Lewis of Mathews County. Christopher Todd Lewis died about 1800 and his estate appears in the 1801 Mathews County Taxable Property List.

Christopher Todd Lewis' father was **John Lewis V of Warner Hall and Mathews County (1728-b1770).** He is Grace's fifth great grandfather. As noted above, John Lewis V married Lucretia Booth about 1748 and they had seven children. That was his second marriage, the first having been to a Joanna Taylor (?), the widow of a Chandler Lewis. John Lewis V was the fifth child of **Col. John Lewis IV of Warner Hall (1694-1754)** and **Frances Fielding (c1702-1731)**. His birth place appears in the *"Abingdon Parish Register"* as Warner Hall in Gloucester County.

Col. John Lewis IV of Warner Hall (1694-1754) was born in St. Peters Parish at *"Chemokins"* in 1694, where he lived during the early years of his life. He later inherited both the *"Chemokins"* estates and Warner Hall from his father **John Lewis III (1669-1725) "the Councilor"**. His marriage about 1718 to Frances Fielding, an only child, brought the Fielding "arms" into the Lewis family (*Argent on a fesse azur three lozenges or.*). The couple produced eight children. In addition to farming, John Lewis IV of Warner Hall was also engaged in shipbuilding and in extensive trade from Warner Hall through the various ports located on the Severn River; and he became an exceptionally wealthy man. He was appointed in 1748 to the Virginia Council, the highest honor a Virginian could achieve politically. His second son was **John Lewis of Abingdon (1723-1727)**, who died quite young. His third son, **Fielding Lewis (1725-1782)**, built the

Fredericksburg "*Kenmore Plantation*". Of particular interest to our pedigree, his fourth son was also named **John Lewis (1728-b1770)** after his deceased second son. *He is our John Lewis V of Warner Hall discussed earlier.*

John Lewis III, "*the Councilor*", married **Elizabeth Warner (1672-1720)**. She was the heir of **Augustine Warner II (1642-1681)** and brought into this union the large estates of Warner Hall. The **Emigrant Augustine Warner Sr. (1610-1674)** arrived in America about 1628 from Norwich, England. He was of "*Royal Descent*" and bore a coat-of-arms (*vert, a cross engrailed or.*). John Lewis III and Elizabeth Warner produced sixteen children, fourteen of whom survived. Two of their sons founded well known Virginia branches of the Lewis family: **Colonel Charles Lewis (1696-1779) of the "Byrd" and Colonel Robert Lewis (1704-1765) of "Belvoir"**. Initially, the couple lived at "*Chemokins*" before moving in 1702 to Warner Hall. It was at "*Chemokins*" that their son, our **John Lewis IV of Warner Hall** was born. This couple became perhaps the wealthiest and most politically powerful family of their time in Virginia.

The father of "*the Councilor*" was **Major/Colonel John Lewis, Jr. (1633-b1690)** the son of the Emigrant John Lewis. He married **Isabella Miller (1640-1704)** about 1665, and they had fifteen children. A son born two years before the "*Councilor*," was **Captain Edward Lewis (1667-1713)**. He is very important to our pedigree and this importance will be discussed in the next chapter. John Lewis, Jr. was the youngest child of the Emigrant and he was the only child of his mother **Catherine Phillip (c1610-b1652)**, the Emigrant's second wife. His birth is recorded in the St. Teilo church "*Parish Register*" in Wales. He immigrated to Virginia in 1653 with his father, the Emigrant, in a party of five. He obtained his own Land Patent for 250 acres in 1655 and then another Land Patent for an additional 1,700 acres in 1663. He was the Executor of the estate of **Major William Lewis (1696-1663)** in 1663, who is believed to be the brother of Johane Lewis, the Emigrant's first wife, and he inherited the "*Chemokins*" estate, also called "*Port Holy*", from William Lewis, receiving the Land Patent for those lands in 1667.

The **Emigrant John Lewis (c1592-1657)** was the father of Major/Colonel John Lewis Jr. (II). He had two wives during his lifetime, but neither was living when he came late in life to America from exile in Barbados in 1653, accompanied by his youngest child by his second wife, John Lewis, Jr., and three others. Neither of his two wives, **Johane Lewis (b1595-b1652) or Catherine Phillip (c1610-b1652)**, were then alive. The Emigrant was a "Royalist" and a Welsh land owner. Oliver Cromwell seized him in Wales, probably at the "*Battle of Chepstow Castle*" during the Civil War (three men with the surname of Lewis were captured there). He was exiled with other "Royalists" to the island of Barbados for two years. From there, he immigrated with four other persons to Virginia in 1653, with his Land Patent and "*head rights*" for 250 acres in New Kent/Gloucester "in hand". His son Major/Colonel John Lewis Jr. accompanied him to Virginia from Barbados. Four years later the Emigrant was buried on his "*head right*" land on Poropotanke Creek in Gloucester County. His tombstone was engraved with the Lewis family coat-of-arms, which he had brought from Monmouthshire, Wales. It goes directly back to the famous Welsh King Rhys Goch, whose coat-of-arms bears the same dragon and bloody hand as that on the tombstone of the Emigrant John Lewis.

CHAPTER FOUR

BACK INTO ANCIENT WALES

The father of the Emigrant was **Lewis ap Richard (aka Prichard and Rycketts) (c1570-1616)**, who married **Catherine Morgan (c1572-1615)**, Llantillo Pertholey Parish. The Emigrant's grandfather was **Richard (Prichard) Lewis the Elder (c1550-1628)** from Llangattock-nigh-Uske in Brecknockshire. The Elder's coat-of-arms was the "*dragons head*" holding in its mouth a "*hand gules*". That is the same "arms" found on the Gloucester tombstone of his grandson the Emigrant John Lewis and the same "arms" belonging to **Rhys Goch, Lord of Ystrad-yw and Ewyas (c960 AD-a990 AD)**, from whom Richard the Elder was descended. Rhys Goch in turn was descended from all six of the "*Royal Tribes of Wales*" listed on the CD. The many generations going back from Richard Lewis the Elder to Rhys Goch are also on the CD.

At this point it is necessary to make an important point concerning the history of ancient Wales. For many generations and centuries the English consciously suppressed the written history of Wales in an effort to dominate the Welsh. The Welsh had their own language, and much of their history has been dependent on oral recitation and memory. However, the "*Triads*" are one written historical source document that has been used by Welsh historians, and their translation has been very important. All of this has confused the chronology and the accuracy of dates in Welsh history. One Welsh historian has even stated that all dates in Welsh history are in error by thirty years. This confusion is reflected in the Welsh dates found on the CD. The names of the individuals and the proper placement of their relationships are believed to be reasonably accurate, but the dates in many instances are not confirmed and are frequently forced. The selected dates are generally in line with the criteria set out in the introduction.

The father of Rhys Goch was **Lord Maenarch ap Griffin (c930 AD-a 975 AD)**, Lord of Brecknock. He was fourteenth in descent from a famous knight who was Grace's 37th great grandfather, a "*Battle Knight*" who sat on the "*Roundtable*" of **King Arthur II (c495 AD-c579 AD) the Liberator and Emperor**. His name is **Caradawg Freichfras (c510 AD-546 AD) Lord of Brycheiiniog**, and his coat-of-arms is "*a sable a chevron between three spear heads, embrued gules*". Caradawg Freichfras was known throughout Wales as "*strong arm*" or "*brawny arm*". He died in the "*Battle at Cattraeth*" in 546 AD, a battle in which 360 knights died and only three knights survived. Caradawg Freichfras was a nephew of King Arthur II, who was also known as the "*Uthyr Pendragon III*". King Arthur II was Grace's 40th great grand uncle. During his lifetime he was married to three women, each of them were named Lady Gwenhwyfar (Guinevere) The story of "why three queens?" is related on the CD and is based on the "Welsh Triads" Arthurian research. King Arthur II was assassinated in 579 AD and he was initially buried at Coed y Mwstyr in Glamorgan. Later, he was reburied in the "*Cave of Pavillions*" in the "*Forest of Mystery*". The descendents of Caradawg Freichfras became rulers of Breconshire and Wales. Caradawg Freichfras was the "*Cadwr Earl of Cornwall (Battle Knight)*" cited in the "Welsh Triads" and he was the Lord of Gloucester and Fferlis. Caradawg Freichfras' mother was **Gwen Brychan born about 490AD.** She is Grace's thirty-eighth great-grandmother and is of particular interest to our pedigree.

Gwen Brychan's paternal grandfather was **Prince Anlach born about 440 AD,** a member of the Irish royal family. His father was **King Coromac of Ireland born about 420 AD,** and his grandfather was **King Brusc born about 390 AD.** Gwen Brychan's father was **Brychan Brycheiniog, born about 480 AD,** and her paternal grand mother was **Queen Marcel born about 475 AD.** She was the sister of King Arthur II. Queen Marcel's ancestral line goes back to **King Arch (Archwyn), born about 50 BC** in ancient Wales. He was the first king of the Apostolic Era and he was Grace's sixtieth great grandfather. Gwen Brychan's pedigree includes such names as **King Ceri Hir Llyngwyn born about 10 BC,** who is buried at Hen Eylwys; **King Llyr-Lediath born about 30 AD,** who cleared Wales of all Romans; **King Bran (b50 AD-80 AD)** *"the blessed",* who founded the Celtic Church in South Wales in 58 AD; **King Crair-Cairlawn (c260 AD-c300 AD) "Carusius the Emperor"** and also known as the *"Dragon of Gwent",* who defeated the Romans and burned down London in 300 AD, regaining Welsh independence; **King Casner Wledig (c280 AD-a310 AD) "Caeser the Leader",** who fought against Constantine the Great's generals; **King Ninniaw ap Erbin (c340 AD-370 AD),** a famous warrior king known as *"St. Ninnian";* and importantly, **King Theodosius Teithfallt born about 370 AD,** who united the British and Roman lines of this pedigree with his marriage to **Teitfall born about 390 AD;** and **Emperor Theodoric Tewdrig (c430 AD-509 AD),** King of South Wales. He was also known as the *"Uther Pendragon I"* and was King Arthur II's grandfather. He was Grace's 42d great grandfather. He was mortally wounded at a *"Battle at a Ford"* and is buried at Mathern in Gwent. These ancestral lines run from Gwen Brychan's father and paternal grandmother.

The mother of Emperor Theodoric Tewdrig was **Teitfal, born about 390 AD,** whose marriage to King Theodosius Teithfallt connected her Roman line with his British line. Her paternal great grandfather was **King Theodore Arthur, "the Conqueror", born about 355 AD.** *"The Conqueror"* seized all of Western Europe and was the King of Greece. He was Grace's forty-sixth great-grandfather. His grandfather was the **Emperor of the West, Magnus Clemens Maximas (324 AD-c388 AD).** Maximas commanded a Roman army in Britain, where he defeated the Scots and the Picts in 381 AD. Next, he conquered Gaul on the continent and invaded Italy in 387 AD. After several battles in Italy, Emperor Theodosious captured him and he was executed in Rome in 388 AD. The grandfather of Maximas was the **British Emperor Constantine the Great (c265 AD-a324 AD),** who by 324 AD was *"master of the entire Roman Empire".* He was Grace's 50th great grandfather. It's interesting to note that these two Welsh branches of the pedigree that were united by the marriage of Theodosius Teithfallt and Teitfal in the early fifth century (the British and the Roman lines in ancient Wales), waged war against each other in the third and fourth centuries. The *"Dragon of Gwent",* King Crair-Caerlawn, defeated the Romans and burned London in 300 AD; and King Casner Wledig, *"Caeser the Leader",* fought Constantine the Great's generals. The CD traces this Roman line of Teitfal back to **Claudius II (c196 AD-270 AD).** Constantine the Great's mother was **Empress Helena, "Saint", who was born about 240 AD.** She discovered the *"True Cross"* in her journeys to the East and brought it back with her to Britain, where it's believed to be bricked up in a cave in Nevern. Her father was **King Coel Hen (c218 AD-**

c303 AD), who was the King of Colchester and the "*Old King Cole*" of nursery rhyme fame. He was Grace's 52nd great grandfather.

"TREE VIEW" OF

KING BRYCHAN BRYCHEINIOG

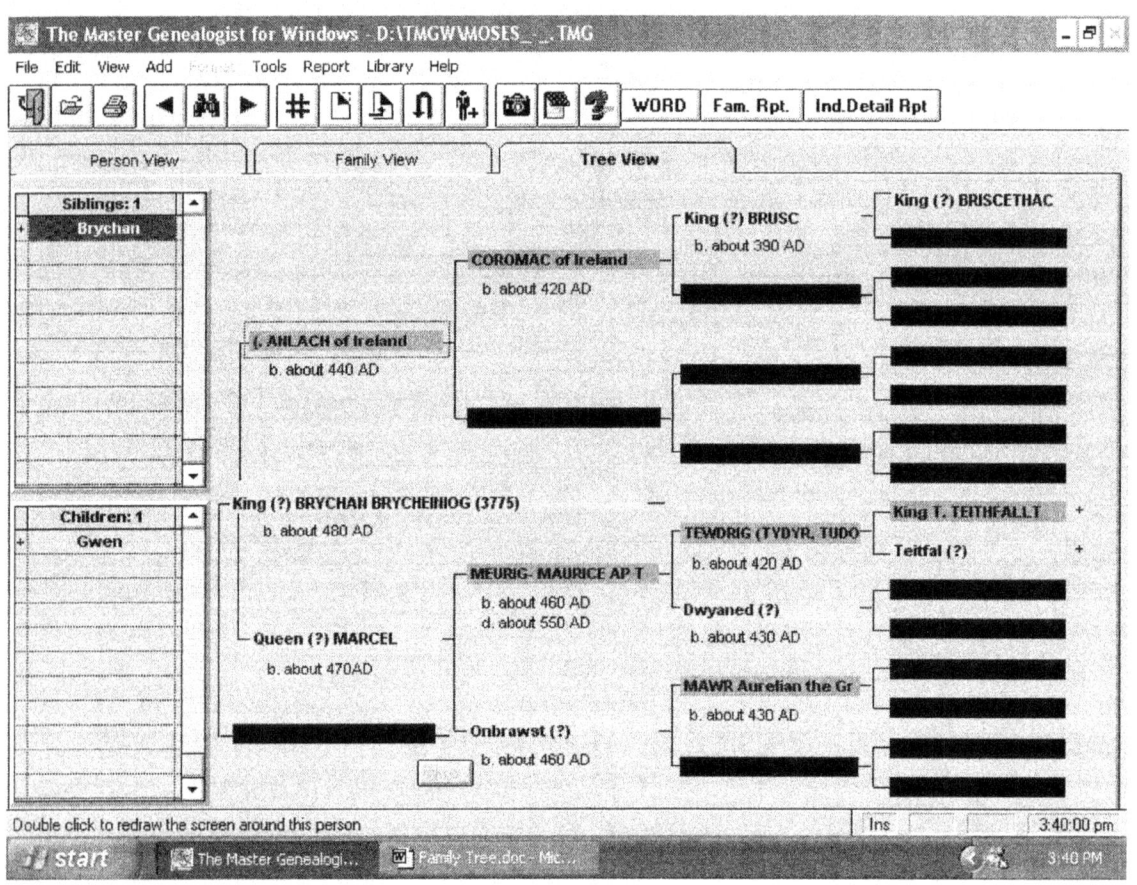

CHAPTER FIVE

A MATERNAL LINE TO THE EMIGRANT JOHN LEWIS

In Chapter 2 George Washington Lewis was identified as the central person in a double line going back to the Emigrant John Lewis. That chapter dealt with a paternal line that began with George Washington Lewis' father John Lewis of Mathews County. His mother, Mary Whiting Hubard, was the daughter of **James Burwell Hubard, Jr, (c1760-)** and **Mary (Mollie) Whiting (1756-)**, both of Gloucester County. She was Grace's third great grandmother. Mary (Mollie) Whiting's parents were **Captain John Whiting (1734-1790)** and **Mary Perrin (1738-1787)**. The Whitings were an old established Virginia family founded by the **Emigrant James Whiting (c1628-)** who established himself on the North River of Gloucester County in 1642, after immigrating on the ship *"The George"* at the early age of nine. His family home, *"Elmington Plantation"*, was occupied by several Whiting generations. The Emigrant James Whiting brought to Virginia a coat-of-arms of three leopard's heads around a chevron. Captain John Whiting, Mary (Mollie) Whiting's father, was a captain in the militia of Gwynn's Island in Mathews County. He was also a county Sheriff, a delegate to the Virginia Assembly, and a Gloucester County delegate to the Convention. Captain John Whiting's mother, Mary Perrin, grew up on a Sarah's Creek plantation known as *"Little England"*, across the creek from where the Lewis family lived. Mary's parents were **Captain John Perrin Jr. (1721-)** and **Mary Booth (b1785-)**. The Perrin family was also an old established family that was founded in Virginia by the **Emigrant John Perrin (c1645-)**, who is Grace Moses' ninth great grandfather. Her seventh great grandmother, **Elizabeth Throckmorton (1698-1728)**, married **Captain John Perrin Sr. (1690-1752)** in about 1715. The CD takes the Throckmorton family back to **Gabriel Throckmorton (c1529-)**, who is of *"Blood Royal"* descent. The family's emigrant was **John Throckmorton (1633-1678)**. His coat-of-arms description is lengthy, and it is found on the CD.

Captain John Whiting's parents were **Colonel Beverly Whiting (c1707-1755)** and **Mary Skaife (c1715-b1755)**. Beverly Whiting, lived at *"Elmington Plantation"*, which he had inherited from his father **Colonel Henry Whiting (1680-1728)**. He was a Burgess for fourteen years from 1740-1754 in Gloucester County. Captain John Whiting's mother was **Mary Skaife (c1715-b1755)**, and his paternal grandmother was **Ann Lewis (1689-1716)**, who married the **Emigrant John Skaife (c1682-1786)** about 1711. This lady was the daughter of **Captain Edward Lewis (1667-1713)**, who we noted in Chapter 3 was a son of the Emigrant John Lewis. It was also noted that Captain Edward Lewis was the brother of John Lewis III, *"the Councilor"*, of Warner Hall. Both men, sons of Major/Colonel John Lewis Jr., were grandsons of the Emigrant John Lewis. These two family ancestral lines to the Emigrant began with the parents of our George Washington Lewis and met with the two brothers, John Lewis III and Captain Edward Lewis, both of whom were Grace's great-grandfathers. The roots of these two ancestral lines to the Emigrant outlined in Chapter 3 are identical back into ancient Wales.

CHAPTER SIX

A CONNECTION TO THE WASHINGTON FAMILY

Returning briefly to Chapter 2, we note that our George Washington Lewis married a lady named **Elizabeth Frances Spann (1795-1834),** who was Grace's 2nd great grandmother. Elizabeth's parents were **Daniel Spann (1773-c1817)** and **Jane Thornton (c1778-c1815).** The CD has three earlier generations of the Spann family. However, it is Elizabeth Frances Spann's mother, Jane Thornton, who is of particular interest to us now, because Jane Thornton's mother was **Jane Washington (c1744-).** This lady's father was **Augustine Washington II (1720-1762)** of "Wakefield", and his father, **Augustine Washington I (1694-1743)**, was President George Washington's father and Grace's 6th great grandfather. The CD goes back four previous Washington family generations to an early **Laurence Washington (c1568-1616).** Jane Washington's paternal great grandmother was **Mildred Warner who was born about 1675**. Mildred was married to **Laurence Washington (1659-1698)** and her mother was **Mildred Reade (1642-1692).** Mildred was also the granddaughter of our Emigrant George Reade noted in chapter 2. So let us now explore the Emigrant George Reade's important connection to the Windebank and Dymoke families in England that was introduced in chapter 2.

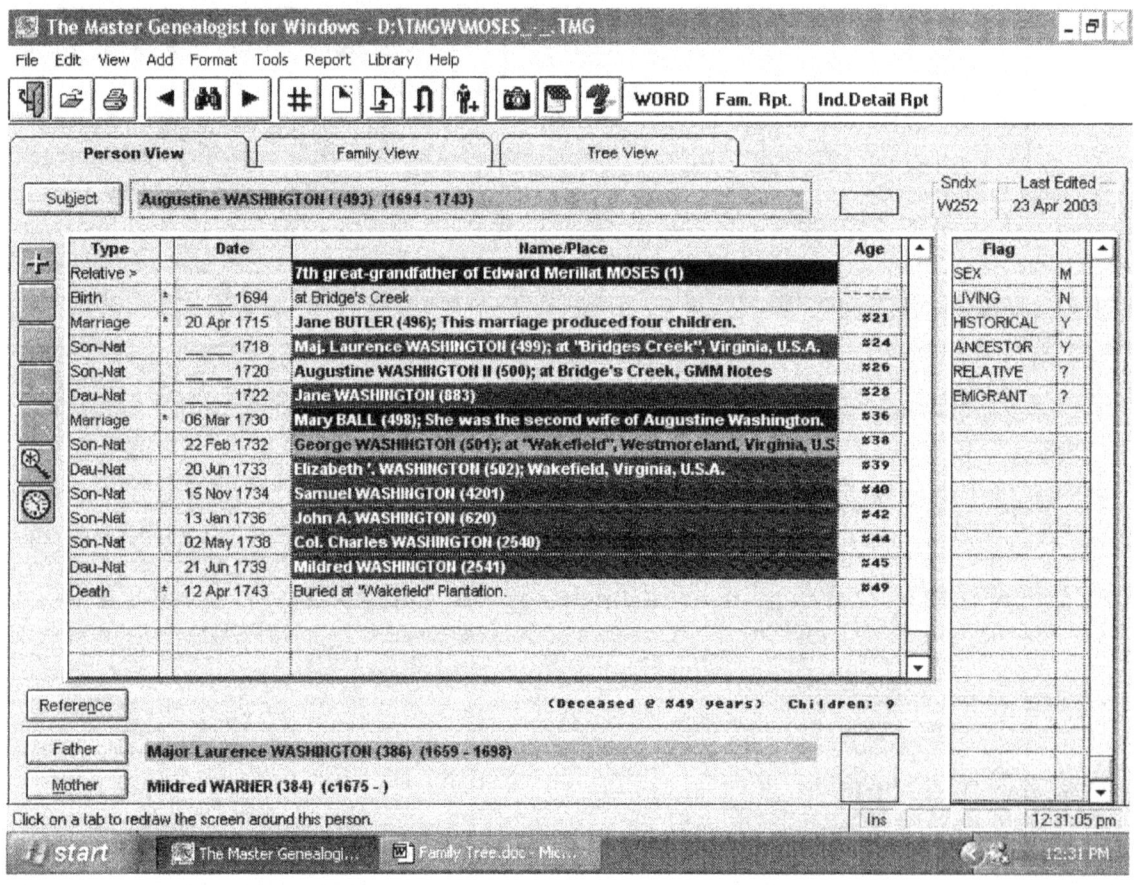

CHAPTER SEVEN

THE DYMOKE AND GASCOIGNE FAMILIES

In chapter 2 the Emigrant George Reade's paternal genealogy was discussed on page 19. His mother was **Mildred Windebank (1584-a1630)**, and her parents were **Sir Thomas Windebank, Knight (c1550-1607)** and **Lady Frances Dymoke (c1550-)**. Sir Thomas Windebank was knighted at Whitehall in 1603. He was the *"Clerk of the Signet"* to Queen Elizabeth and *"Deputy Clerk of the Privy Council"*. Lady Frances Dymoke's parents were **Sir Edward Dymoke, Knight of Scrivelsby, Lincoln (c1490-1566)** and **Lady Anne Tailboys (Talvois) (c1498-a1563)**. There are three additional generations of Dymokes on the CD back to 1406 AD.

Sir Edward Dymoke was descended from Robert Marmyon and Rollo the Dane. He inherited the Scrivelsby estates that had originally been given to Marmyon by **William the Conqueror (1025-1087)**, Grace's 25th great grandfather. These estates were subsequently bequeathed within the Dymoke family over several generations. Edward Dymoke was the *"champion"* for King Edward Sixth, Queen Mary, and Queen Elizabeth, and he was the hereditary *"Champion of England"*. Edward's father Robert was also the *"Kings Champion"*, and he was present at Runnemede with another son, Robert Dymoke, Jr.

Lady Anne Tailboys' paternal line on the CD goes back seven generations to **William Tailboys (c1307-)**. The Tailboys were early members of Parliament and sheriffs in Lincolnshire. Anne Tailboys mother was **Lady Elizabeth Gascoigne (c1470-1559)**, whose paternal ancestral lines include the family names De Neville, De Ferrers, and Newmarch of Wormsley. She was Grace's eleventh great grandmother. Elizabeth Gascoigne's father was **Sir William Gascoigne, Knight of Gawthorpe, York (c1436-a1470)**, a descendent of **King Edward III (1312-1377)**.

Elizabeth's Gascoigne's maternal ancestral lines include the names of Percy, Poynings, De Mortimer, De Neville, Beaufort, Marshall, De Clare and the several Edwards, Kings of England. Her great, great grandmother was **Joan Beaufort (c1376-1440)**, whose grandfather was King Edward III of England. He was Grace's 17th great grandfather. So Elizabeth Gascoigne was a descendent of King Edward III on both her father's and mother's lines. The Percys were the Earls of Northumberland. **Sir Henry "Harry Hotspur" Percy (1366-1403)** was a well known member of this English family. There are several generations of De Mortimers on the CD. **Roger De Mortimer, 8th Baron of Wigmore, (1287-1330)**, was the *"King's Lieutenant"* in Ireland in 1316 and the *"Earl of March"* in 1328. **Earl William Marshall (1146-1219)** was the *"greatest Knight in Europe"*. He was the 3rd Earl of Pembroke through his marriage to **Isabel De Clare (c1172-1220)**. He was the *"Kings Champion"* and the *"Protector of the Realm"* in 1216-1219 and was named in the Magna Charta in 1215. William Marshall was Grace's 22nd great grandfather. These families are all well known English royalty. The emigrant George Reade brought much to *"My Family Tree"*.

"TREE VIEW" OF

ELIZABETH GASCOIGNE

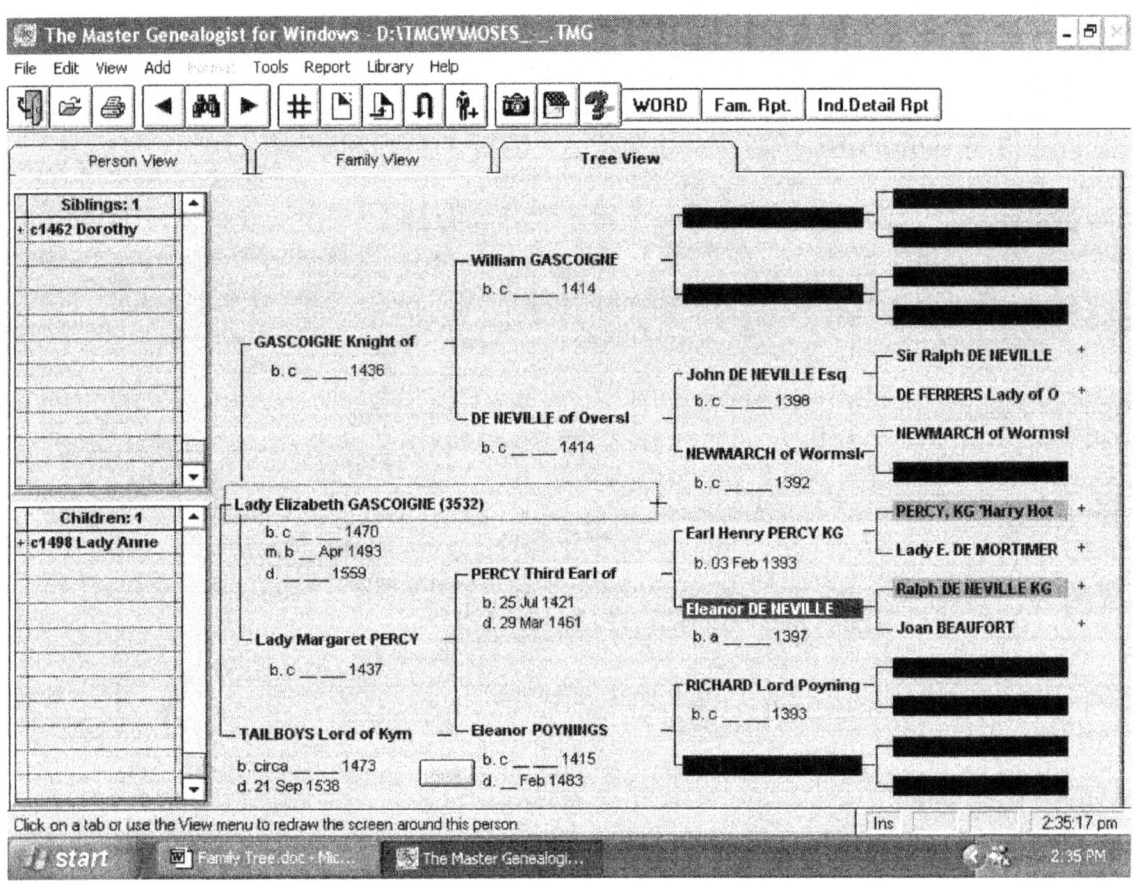

CHAPTER EIGHT

PEDIGREE BRANCHES INTO

IRELAND

In Chapter 3 we briefly mentioned Prince Anlach of Ireland, a paternal grandfather of Gwen Brychan, who was Graces's 38th great grandmother in Wales. Prince Anlach's wife was **Queen Marcel born about 470 AD**. She was the daughter of the **Emperor Marcian Meurig-Maurice ap Twedrig (c450 AD-550 AD)**, the King of Gwent and South Wales. Queen Marcel was also the older sister of King Arthur II, the Liberator and Emperor in Wales, whose *"Roundtable"* is well known and documented. This marriage of Queen Marcel and Prince Anlach united the Irish Royal House with the lines of the ancient Welsh kings. Prince Anlach was the son of the reigning King of Ireland, **King Coromac who was born about 420AD**. The CD line goes back to **King Briscethac who was born about 360 AD**.

SCOTLAND

King Henry I (1070-1135), Henry Beauclerc, ruled England from 1100-1135 when he succeeded to the throne upon the death of his brother William Rufus who ruled from 1087-1100. He was the second son of **William I, the Conqueror (1025-1087)**. King Henry I was an ancestor of King Edward III and was Grace's 24th great grandfather. King Henry married **Queen Matilda of Scotland (1079-1118)**, a widow and Empress of the Holy Roman Empire by marriage. She was sometimes known as Edith. Her father was **King Malcolm III Canmore, King of Scotland (1031-1093)** and her mother was **Queen Margaret, Saint Margaret of Scotland (1046-1093)**. Queen Margaret's paternal line goes back to the famous Saxon **King Alfred the Great (849 AD-901 AD)**. King Malcolm III's paternal line goes back three generations on the CD to **King Kenneth II MacMalcolm, King of Scots (c957 AD-994 AD)**, Grace's 28th great grandfather.

FRANCE

William I (The Conqueror) was the Duke of Normandy in France in 1035. He married **Princess Matilda of Flanders (1032-1083)** in 1053. This lady, known also as *"Maude of Flanders"*, was a Flemish princess, and she was Grace's 25th great grandmother. Princess Matilda's paternal line goes back through seven generations of *"Counts of Flanders"* to **Baldwin I, Bran de Fer (c842 AD-879 AD)**. His wife **Judith (c846 AD-c865 AD)** was the daughter of **Charles II, the Bald (c805 AD-877AD)**, whose father was **Emperor Louis I (c780 AD-840 AD)**. The father of Louis I was **Emperor**

Charlemagne (747 AD-814 AD), the King of the Franks from 768 AD-814 AD. He was given the title of *"Augustus"* by Pope Leo III in 800 AD. Emperor Charlemagne was a famous warrior king, and his empire included France, Italy, the Baltic, most of Austria and Prussia, and part of Turkey. He was Grace's 35th great grandfather.

A second important pedigree line into France starts with the second wife of **King Edward I of England (1239-1307),** known as "Longshanks", **Queen Marguerite of France (c1275-1317).** She was Grace's 21st great grandmother. Her father was **King Philippe III (1245-1285) King of France** and her grandfather was **King Louis IX (1215-1270).** The CD goes back through ten more generations of French kings to **King Robert I (c895 AD-923 AD).**

"PERSON VIEW" OF

KING EDWARD I OF ENGLAND, "LONGSHANKS"

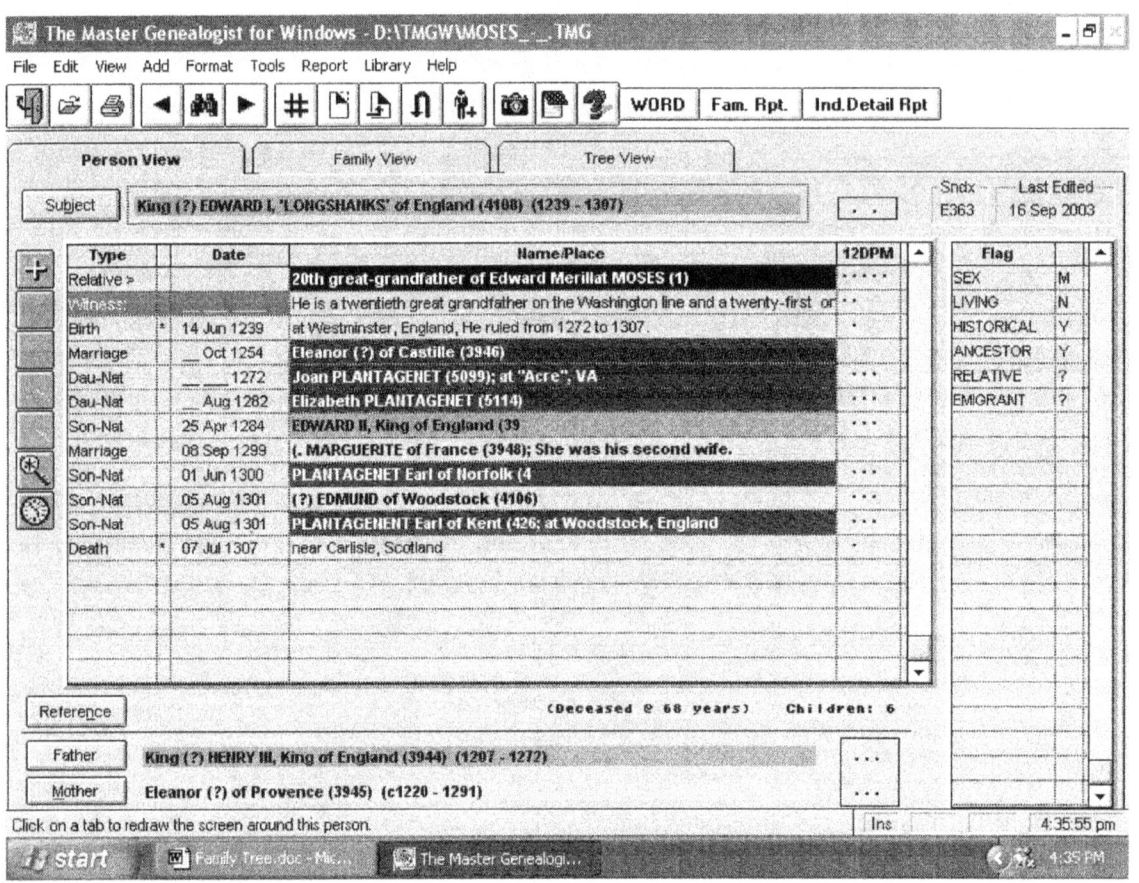

CHAPTER NINE

"TREE LIMBS" WITH HISTORICAL PERSONS

IN AMERICA

Present in this "family tree" are three presidents of the United States. First, and mentioned previously, is **President George Washington (22 Feb 1732-14 Dec 1799)** the leader of America's Revolutionary War Army and America's first president. He is Grace's 5th great-grand uncle, and the son of **Augustine Washington I (1694-12 Apr 1792),** who resided at *"Wakefield Plantation"* on Pope's Creek in Westmoreland County. Augustine Washington is Grace's 6th great grandfather. Because George Washington had no children, there are no direct descendents of America's first president. The emigrant **Colonel John Washington (1627-1677)** was President George Washington's great grandfather, who came to Virginia in 1656 in order to escape Oliver Cromwell's puritan England, after first fighting for Charles I. The royalist Washington family is of *"Blood Royal"* descent. The second president in this "family tree" is **President Thomas Jefferson (27 Apr 1743-1826)**, Grace's second cousin 6 times removed. He was America's third elected president and the author of the *"Declaration of Independence"*. He made his home at *"Monticello"*, a plantation near Charlottesville. Thomas Jefferson's mother was **Jane Randolph (1720-1757)** and his great grandmother was **Mary Isham born after 1644**. Both the Randolph and the Isham families were descendents of *"Blood Royal"*. The third president in this "family tree" is **President William Henry Harrison born about 1742**, Grace's third cousin 6 times removed. His father was **Benjamin Harrison, who was born about 1690.** He lived in *"Berkeley"* in Charles City County. Benjamin Harrison was a signer of the *"Declaration of Independence"*. President William Harrison's mother was **Elizabeth Bassett born about 1742**. Her grandmother was **Elizabeth Armistead (c1673-b1716)**. The Armistead family emigrant was **William Armistead (1610-c1660),** who came to Elizabeth City after receiving large land grants in 1635 that were among the first in Gloucester County. The Armisteads built and lived at *"Hesse Plantation"* and intermarried with the Robinson and Lee families. William Armistead was Grace's 9th great grandfather, and the family is of *"Blood Royal"* descent.

Thomas Nelson (1677-1745), a 6th great grandfather, also bore a Coat-of-Arms when he emigrated from Penrith, England. He founded the town of Yorktown, where he built the first Custom House, one of the earliest brick buildings in the state. The Nelson family intermarried with the Grymes, Armistead, Randolph, Beverly, and Burwell families.

Anne Tilney (a1648-b1736), a 7th great grandmother, was the daughter of **Anne Smith,** *of "Jamestowne Society"*, **who was born about 1632** and **John Tilney (1618-1700)**, who emigrated in 1639 and was appointed a Justice in Accomack County. They were both 8th great grandparents. The Tilney family goes back four generations on the CD and the Smith (Smyth) family goes back five generations. The Smith Coat-of-Arms was granted to John Smyth and his issue by the Queen. His son, **Customer Thomas Smyth (b1538-b1591)**, was the *"Customer of London"* during Queen Elizabeth's reign, collecting duties and subsidies for inbound and outbound cargo from London.

Still another ancestor of *"Blood Royal"* descent was the emigrant **Colonel William Randolph (1650-1711)**, who settled at *"Turkey Island"* on the James River in Henrico County. He was Grace's 7th great grandfather. Colonel Randolph helped found *William and Mary College*. He was a Burgess and was elected "Speaker" of the House of Burgesses in 1698. He served on the "Council" and was also the Attorney General of the Colony. The Randolph family intermarried with the Wormley, Cary, Jefferson, Isham, and Beverly families.

Sarah Ludlow (b1638-a1668), an 8th great grandmother, married the emigrant **Colonel John Carter (1620-1669)**. One of their sons was **"King" Robert Carter (1663-1732)** of *"Carotoman"*. He was one of the most prominent Virginians of his day and was a Justice, a Burgess, a member of the "Council", and a 7th great grandfather.

There are many Throckmortons in this "family tree", and they too are descended from *"Blood Royal"*. Their emigrant was **John Throckmorton (1633-1678)**, Grace's 9th great grandfather. The Throckmortons intermarried with the Lewis family and the Cooke family, which was founded by the **Emigrant Mordecai Cooke (c1645-a1675)**.

The emigrant **Captain Thomas Smith born about 1618** was Grace's 9th great grandfather. He emigrated in 1634 in the ship *"Jon and Dorothy"* and was brought to America by **Adam Thoroughgood (1603-b1640)**, a 10th great grandfather. Adam Thoroughgood also bore a coat-of-arms from England. He was a Burgess and later was a member of the "Council" from Princess Ann County in 1637. Thomas Smith received two large "Land Patents" for 600 acres in the *"Jamestown Colony"*.

Ann Lovelace (c1610-1652) is Grace's 10th great grandmother. She is in the family's *"Magna Charta"* and *"Charlemagne"* lines and is a descendent of *"Blood Royal"*. She was the daughter of **Sir William Lovelace II (1584-1627)**. She married the **Reverend John Gorsuch (c1608-1657)** and they had eleven children.

The emigrant **Colonel Richard Lee (c1609-c1664)** bore a Coat-of-Arms from Shropshire, England, when he immigrated to America in 1640. He was a member of the Privy Council and was also Secretary of State. He was a Burgess and a Justice and a 10th great grandfather. **General Robert Edward Lee (1807-1870), C.S.A.**, Grace's 3d cousin five times removed was Richard Lee's descendent. The Lee family intermarried with the Carter, Custis, Grymes, and Bland families.

Grace's 11th great grandfather was **Sir George Yeardley (c1580-1627)** who was married to **Temperence Flowerdew (c1582-b1630)**. Sir Yeardley was appointed Governor of the Virginia Colony in 1618, and in 1619 he summoned the first legislative assembly ever convened in America. He too is of *"Blood Royal"* descent.

CHAPTER 10

THE MOSES GENEALOGICAL RECORD

While Grace Moses was understandably preoccupied with her own ancestors in Virginia, she did outline a major trunk of the Moses family tree beginning with her husband **Merillat Moses (1909-1988).** Her information was principally extracted from an excellent two volume genealogical record that was written and published by Mr. Zebina Moses in 1890 and in 1906. This data was enhanced by Grace's personal knowledge of the most recent three generations of Moses' family members, their spouses, and their children. Also, in the past two years a 1st cousin of Merillat Moses who lives in Pennsylvania, Howard R. Moses, has contributed additional information from his examination of the Moses genealogy over several years.

The family emigrant was **John Moses (c1610-a1661) of Plymouth and Duxbury, MA**. He came to America to establish a ship building business in the Massachusetts Bay Colony, and then in Plymouth and Duxbury as early as 1639. There was a real need to fill "a demand for men who could build ships" in a land that had plentiful timber for building ships.

A son of John Moses of Plymouth and Duxbury was **John Moses II (c1632-1683) of Windsor and Simsbury**, who established his own ship building business. It was this John Moses who married **Mary Brown (c1633-1689)** on May 18, 1653. **Peter Brown (c1610-) of Windsor** was her father, and it was his family that was noted in the histories that were written by the historians Stiles, Phelps, and Brown as being of *Mayflower line descent*. The Stiles book *"History of Windsor"* also noted that the Moses family was not Puritan, and in fact they were strong supporters of the Church of England.

The Foster family intermarried with the Moses family in Massachusetts and there are many from the Foster family on the CD, compliments of Howard R. Moses' research. The **Emigrant Sergeant Thomas Foster (c1600-1682)** came to America in 1634 with his brother William, in the ship *"Hercules"*.

There are some interesting branches in this Moses record. One branch consists of several generations of the Swiss French Huegenot family "Merillat". The family emigrant from Switzerland was **David Adolph Merillat (c1803-1839)**, whose son **Charles Henry Merillat (c1825-1897)** married **Mary Margaret Sioussat (c1828-1897)** about 1842. Her father was **Jean Pierre Sioussat (1781-1864),** and there is considerable family oral history indicating that he was of French royal blood, and was evacuated as a young child to England to ensure his safety during the vicious aftermath of the French Revolution. His name has been orally connected with that of the famous French minister Talleyrand. As a young adult he was sent to America with *"Letters of Introduction"* and quickly was appointed the Majordomo at the White House, where he became a *confidante* of Dolly Madison, the president's wife. He was nicknamed "French John", and it was he who saved the Gilbert Stuart White House portrait of George Washington when the British burned Washington, by moving it to a local farmhouse where it remained until the "White House" was rebuilt. The original price of that portrait was $800. After the War of 1812, because of the high level of trust in which "French John" was held, he was appointed courier of routine U.S. Government gold shipments between Washington and Philadelphia.

During a trip to Wales in 1983, Grace discovered some evidence that the Emigrant John Moses' family came from Monmouthshire and the town of Abergevenney in Wales. This was a real coincidence, because we know that Grace's own emigrant ancestor John Lewis also came from Monmouthshire and immigrated to Gloucester County, Virginia, twenty years later. The Moses' Coat-of-Arms from Wales is "*Gules, a chevron between three cocks*" and the Motto is "*Dum Spiro Spero*" (While I breathe I hope).

CHAPTER 11

A SUMMARY OF THIS PEDIGREE'S ODYSSEY

Tracking Grace McLean Moses pedigree has taken us on a wonderful odyssey from Virginia to Britain. With the help of a computer and a fine genealogy program, much has been discovered that even Grace may not have been aware of. Her work has taken us back into ancient Wales, Ireland, and Scotland, into England, and over the English Channel to France and Italy. Since a genealogical study such as this is really never completed, at some point it's important to summarize the pedigree, catch our breath, and then continue on. This book is such a summary of this pedigree. However, while many questions have been answered, there are clearly several major unanswered questions. The answers to these questions must result from additional research and work after this book is published, and these answers will contribute to a further understanding of this pedigree. Three major unanswered questions are:

1. What are the roots back into Scotland of the **Emigrant Lauchlin McLean (c1786-1855)**? Correspondence by Grace was unable to identify his McLean parents in Scotland. While clearly he came from the Highland "Clan McLean" when he immigrated to Nova Scotia, that clan was unable to provide any requested information. Additional research on this line might be very productive.

2. The **Emigrant John Moses of Plymouth and Duxbury (c1610-a1661)** line back into Wales is an area that could be very interesting with additional research. Is it possible that the Lewis and the Moses lines crossed in Wales or England in the seventeenth century?

3. How far back into Ireland does the family pedigree go from **Prince Anlach, born about 440AD** and his father **King Coromac, born about 420AD?** Does this line go back to the "*Holy Grail*", and the "*Stone of Scone*" upon which British kings are traditionally crowned? This could be a very exciting addition to the pedigree!

There are other questions that are self evident and that are of considerable interest. At some point they will be answered! The "tree" continues to grow.

USING YOUR "FAMILY TREE" *read only* CD

1. There are six family folders containing images of documents, pictures and correspondence linked to individuals in the *The Master Genealogist* (TMG) and in the *Second Site* programs. Click on the appropriate CD "icon" to access these images directly. If you use a **TMG (version 4.0d)** program in a D-Drive "partition" on your hard drive, these images, which are all linked by D-Drive paths, may be viewed through TMG, otherwise these image links must be viewed by clicking on the CD's **tmg5setup** "icon", and using **TMG version 5**.

2. There is a CD GEDCOM folder for computer users who use a genealogy program other than TMG. Click on "**Data-File.GED**" and select "**Word Pad**".

3. The program *Second Site* requires no computer genealogy program, compliments of www.johncardinal.com. To open this program, double click on "**Second Site**" and click on "**Second Site.exe**". Click on "**File**"; then click on "**Open**" and highlight "**Second Site.sdf**"; Click on "**Open**" and click on "**File**" again. Then click on "**Browse**", and *slowly* navigate as it's very "mouse" sensitive.

4. The **tmg5setup** "icon" opens the **TMG version 5 (read only) "30 day program"**. To restore the **Backup Project 5** data set to the program, first open "**TMG version 5**" by clicking on the **tmg5setup** "icon", and immediately select the "**Sample**" data set. This permits you to click on "**File**" and then "**Restore**" of the **Backup Project 5** data. Most of your System Configuration settings should not be changed, but check to be sure. The "**Flag Manager**" and the "**Accent**" colors are both under "**File**". Also check the "**Automatic Relationship Calculator**".

5. There is a **Backup 4d** data set for computer users who use **The Master Genealogist Version 4.0d.** This data must be "**Restored**" if used with **TMG 4.0d**. If used in **TMG version 5**, this data must be "**Imported**". When the data is "**Restored**" to **TMG 4.0d, the System Configurations** probably must be reset:
    a. Recheck the "**Automatic Relationship Calculator**" (Tools-Options-Tags) and insert the person ID# 3. This is the ID of Grace McLean Moses.
    b. Recheck your "**Flags**": (click on File-Customize-Flags).
    c. Recheck your flag "**Accent**" colors (click on Tools-Accent Definition):
        (1) **Ancestor**: Yellow with Black print
        (2) **Historical**: Brown w/White print
        (3) **Relative**: Red w/White print
        (4) **Emigrant**: Green w/Black print
        (5) **Conflict** (two or more attributes): Aqua w/ Black print

6. There is a **Word** document on the CD that contains this book "*My Family Tree*".

For TMG users, the TMG Help Desk is at 410-715-2260 or www.whollygenes.com

www.ingramcontent.com/pod-product-compliance
Lightning Source LLC
Chambersburg PA
CBHW081356230426
43667CB00017B/2851